I want to dedicate this book to a woman that I can say has been the best paradigm of what faithfulness is all about. I watched this woman stand by her man for 43 years and show selfless acts of mercy to her children. When we were sick… I can still hear her prayers of healing in the wee hours of the morning. When we were afraid… I can hear her songs of God and about Jesus that would calm our fears. When we needed someone to hold I could feel her warmth and strong arms surrounding us.

I recall so many memories of this woman's prayer power and word power. I could honestly say that if it hadn't been for this Godly woman my father would not know the Lord today and probably wouldn't be writing this dedication right now. That woman is my MOTHER!

Mom when writing the chapter on Rebekah I thought of you. Mom I love you!

I also want to recognize another dedicated woman who I'm also grateful to and who has shown great faithfulness to her husband and children. If it wasn't for this woman's prayers and love my wonderful wife would not be with me today… that woman is my second mother! Connie thanks for being so strong and faithful to your husband and children. I love you as well!

DOGMAN

God's Unwavering Faithfulness

by

Bishop Jerry A. Grillo, Jr.

ISBN 0-9710967-3-2
Copyright 2002 By Bishop Jerry A. Grillo, Jr.
P.O. Box 3707
Hickory, NC. 28603

"For you, O Lord, will bless the righteous; with favor you will surround him as with a shield." Psalms 5:12

Preface

You have not picked up this book by accident. We are about to enter into one of the greatest subjects written in the Word of God, God's **faithfulness!**

Covenant is a word that isn't used in today's vernacular. Man's word doesn't mean a thing anymore. That's why there are written contracts and documentation. You can't trust anyone to live up to what they have agreed to do. We wonder why society is so untrustworthy.

I had a friend tell me one time that the definition of integrity was *"keeping one's commitment even after the circumstances have changed."* After hearing that, it doesn't seem that many people walk in integrity. People will change what they meant to accommodate their safety and take no care at what it will do to their integrity. I have a pastor friend who lives in Jacksonville, Florida Dr. Dan White. I've nicknamed him the ICEMAN. He calls his men's ministry or leadership training I.C.E. **(Integrity, Character and Excellence) I.C.E.** *This is what the body of Christ needs, a revival in integrity, character and excellence.*

Through these pages you are going to discover that no matter what the circumstances are, God will be faithful to what He has promised. We will laugh, shout and cry together, but at the end we will be convinced to trust this God we serve, without hesitation. As a matter of fact, God never told you to trust man. He said to love men and trust God!

I know and pray that this book will bless you as it has me.

May the Lord shine in your hearts as you do in mine.

Bishop Jerry
F.O.G.MAN

Foreword

Our Christian bookstore shelves are crowded today with so many books by so many authors on an enormous array of subjects that seemingly cover every topic of Christendom. It would seem that the Body of Christ would be healthy and whole with the catastrophic amount of information that is available to the church, but, needless to say, there are still weaknesses, weariness, and wonderers that need a spiritual physician.

One such spiritual physician that I was privileged to meet some time ago is the author of this powerful book. When I met the man I knew it was more than just a casual acquaintance – it was a divine appointment. There are many men of ministry that we meet down through the course of destiny, but not everyone you encounter has the energy of greatness that precedes their introduction or conversation. To meet the man in person, you immediately recognize that he is more than just a man with another message, but he is one who carries the mantle of favor upon his life – appointed and anointed for this season in the Body of Christ. He is a husband, a father, a pastor, teacher, and a scribe with a prescription to challenge you from poverty into prosperity, from fear into faith, and from failure into favor.

My earnest prayer is that as you encounter this manuscript that is before you the words will leap from these pages with confirmation to the sleeping giants of greatness that are within you, even as John leaped within the womb of Elizabeth at the salutation of Mary.

Now, get ready for an extreme expedition that is sure to take you to the peaks of expectancy as you journey into the pages of promise that will elevate you into your future and ignite the passion to pursue your dreams and desires.

Your future is great!
Bishop Joby R. Brady
The River
Raleigh, North Carolina

Table of Contents

Chapter 1
The Faithfulness
Of God

Have you ever sat down and pondered about this God that you serve? Look at the ages of times past and think about all of the generations that have let God down and have walked according to their own desires and passions, ignoring the very laws of God.

When we read about God's response it is not, in my opinion, the norm. If someone does us wrong we immediately desire **retaliation**. We dream and imagine ways to make the person who hurt us pay. Yet, all through the Word of God we see race after race and nation after nation defying and rebelling... God's response is always a response of love and forgiveness.

What we need to do is go through the Word of God and create a firm foundation of why we should love and appreciate God.

Ps 36:5
5 Thy mercy, O LORD, is in the heavens; and thy faithfulness reacheth unto the clouds. KJV

Ps 89:1-5
I will sing of the Lord's great love forever;
with my mouth I will make your faithfulness known through all generations.
2 I will declare that your love stands firm forever,
that you established your faithfulness in heaven itself.

3 You said, "I have made a covenant with my chosen one, I have sworn to David my servant, 4'I will establish your line forever and make your throne firm through all generations.'" Selah
5 The heavens praise your wonders, O LORD, your <u>faithfulness too</u>, in the assembly of the holy ones. NIV

Ps 89:24
24 My faithful love will be with him, and through my name his horn will be exalted. NIV

Ps 89:30-33
30 "If his sons forsake my law and do not follow my statutes,
31 if they violate my decrees and fail to keep my commands,
32 I will punish their sin with the rod, their iniquity with flogging;
33 but I will not take my love from him, nor will I ever betray my <u>faithfulness</u>. NIV

Before we can move further, we need to define the word faithful.

Webster's Dictionary defines the word "faithful" as

1 keeping faith; maintaining **<u>allegiance; constant; loyal</u>**
2 Marked by or showing a strong sense of duty or responsibility; conscientious
3 **<u>accurate; reliable;   full of faith</u>**,

This dynamic fact about God should set us at ease. God has made an alliance with us. God is loyal and constant. He has made a covenant with us. God is going to take care of those who walk in accordance to His Word. God is faithful!

Heb 13:5
5 God has said, "Never will I leave you; never will I for-sake you." NIV

When the pressures of life seem to be winning and there's nothing left in you to even pray, remember Hebrews 13:5 "God will never leave you; never will he forsake you." Cling to this in times of despair. We are never, ever alone… God is always present helping us, guiding us and encouraging us behind the scenes.

Ps 46:1
1 God is our refuge and strength, an ever-present help in trouble. NIV

When we read the book of Esther in the Bible we never see the name of God mentioned, yet all through the book you can feel and sense God's presence. God was working His plan behind the scenes. He was the one orchestrating the demise of the enemy. It is God who works all things out for our good. Just as He did in Esther's day, so shall He do in our day. Search your memories and you will find that in all of life's trials and tribulations, God has been behind the scene working His plan for our good and His purposes. What an awesome God we serve!

Rom 8:28-
28 And we know that in all things God works for the good of those who love him, who have been called according to his purpose. NIV

The prerequisite to this scripture:

(1) love Him (God), and (2) are called according to His purpose. God has set a mandate in His Word so that if we walk according to it, He will make sure that He works all things out for good. Notice that it doesn't say that all things will be good at all times. No, it says that no matter what, if we love God and if we accept our place in His calling, (Note: we are all called to do something for God) He's going to work things out for goodness sake. It will be good, trust God!

WHAT AN AWESOME GOD WE SERVE! HE IS FAITHFUL!

The F.O.G. is evident in so many aspects. There's the F.O.G. (favor of God) The F.O.G. (fatherhood of God) and now the F.O.G. (faithfulness of God).

Who would have ever thought that an Alabama boy who graduated from high school with a 1.9 G.P.A. and couldn't read very well, would be writing books about God. I serve a miracle-working God. He is definitely the **F.O.G.** to me. He's been faithful when I was not.

It is my desire to take you through the Word of God starting in Genesis all the way through Revelation and show all the situations, people and nations where God showed His faithfulness. At the end of this book I will share my testimony on how faithful God really was to me.

My plan is for you to take this book and build a passion for God, church, and for His Word. In life everybody fails... when you fail - and most likely you will sometime during your life. There will be this uncontrollable urge that will cause you to decide that you will never take, touch or do...

You will most likely find yourself in the middle of the exact thing you swore you would never become. **Don't panic** and run away from God. He's not the one judging you; He's the one forgiving you. God is the one leading you back to truth. **I know the church doesn't always seem to walk in love when someone messes up.** Do me a favor; **don't blame God.** Don't take out on Him what humans do. God is not the one pushing you away. NO! God is the love that's pulling you in.

For all have sinned and have fallen short. There's none righteous, not one. We are all a product of "Grace" and if "Grace" got you out the first time, it will get you out again.

This was the whole reason Paul wrote Romans chapter eight.

Rom 8:1-4
1 therefore, there is now no condemnation for those who are in Christ Jesus,
2 because through Christ Jesus the law of the Spirit of life set me free from the law of sin and death.
3 For what the law was powerless to do in that it was weakened by the sinful nature, God did by sending his own Son in the likeness of sinful man to be a sin offering. And so he condemned sin in sinful man,
4 in order that the righteous requirements of the law might be fully met in us, who do not live according to the sinful nature but according to the Spirit. NIV

If you're a woman reading this book and you had an abortion, or have sinned in some form or fashion; if you're a man who has done things you're ashamed of, the only thing you have to do is turn your heart toward Jesus and confess Him as the Son of God. Believe that He died for your sins and arose from the dead. Confess Him as Lord right now and that's it. "There should be no more condemnation." For he who the Son has set free, is free indeed. **You are free!**

Let's keep healthy doctrine here. I didn't say that if you did something that might cause you consequences that you wouldn't still have to pay for them. I've seen a lot of men in prison get saved, and they are as saved as you and I are. Guess what? They are still serving their sentence. Why? They broke the law and have to pay the consequences for their crime. The good news is that now they are not alone. They have been forgiven and, even though in the natural they have to serve their sentence, they have been freed from their guilt and condemnation. They will not have to pay for their crime or crimes in heaven.

These men at one time had to face the sorrow of their wrong doings, and so did we. Now they have the partnership of God and all His resources to help in times of need. So, don't misunderstand me. God is faithful to His Word and if you have been given a Word, He will be faithful to that Word. It is imperative as a believer that you get in the Word and listen with your spirit, so that you can get a Word to hold onto in times of difficulties.

Chapter 2
Conquering Peer-Pressure
Will Produce
The Faithfulness Of God

This is not going to be an exhaustive study on the faithfulness of God. However, it will be enough to have you running and shouting all the way to church this Sunday.

The first place we need to stop on this journey through the Word is in Genesis chapter 5 through chapter 9.

We read about a man named Noah. Noah's name means... **nuwach** (noo'-akh); a primitive root; **to rest**, i.e. **settle down**; (to dwell, stay, let fall, place, alone, withdraw, give comfort, etc.):

> *Noah Found Favor in the Eyes of The Lord!*

Notice that Noah's name shows us that he was a man of rest. He was settled. His name bears the mark that he was probably a peaceful and good man, one who didn't cause a lot of grief and was always in good spirits. The Bible says that he was a righteous man.

Even though Noah was a good man, he lived among people who were wicked, rebellious and involved in all kinds of sexual sins. They were a people who were running out of control. Man had become a cesspool of lust, hatred, and all other kinds of sin. But, not Noah! Noah stayed peaceful and restful. Noah stayed to himself. The best way to keep from falling into the trap of peer-pressure is to stay away from those who can pressure you to fall. Noah had made up his mind to stay away from the God-haters.

Gen 6:5-8
5 The LORD saw how great man's wickedness on the earth had become, and that every inclination of the thoughts of his heart was only evil all the time. 6 The LORD was grieved that he had made man on the earth, and his heart was filled with pain. 7 So the LORD said, "I will wipe mankind, whom I have created, from the face of the earth—men and animals, and creatures that move along the ground, and birds of the air—for I am grieved that I have made them. "NIV

Gen 6:11-13
11 Now the earth was corrupt in God's sight and was full of violence.
12 God saw how corrupt the earth had become, for all the people on earth had corrupted their ways. NIV

Gen 6:7-8
8 But Noah found favor in the eyes of the LORD.
9 Noah was a righteous man, blameless among the people of his time, and he walked with God. NIV

God was grieved in His heart. Mankind had turned out pretty wicked. Here comes the F.O.G. (faithfulness of God). When God looked down and saw what man had become He decided to wipe out mankind completely. God had made up His mind to not just destroy mankind but every living thing.
God couldn't do it when He looked down and saw this one man, Noah. God's heart was turned and He couldn't com-

pletely wipe out mankind. **"Noah found favor."** Noah found the F.O.G. and the F.O.G. (**Faithfulness of God**) found Noah.

Just think how easy it could have been for God. He could have just erased all His troubles with one word of destruction. Think about it… Jesus would have never had to suffer. He would have never been crucified. All God needed to do was wipe out man and that would have been judgment. Yet there was one man named Noah who had not succumbed to the sins of the populace. He was just a quiet, peaceful man living the best he could for God. When God saw him He was reminded that no matter how bad mankind seemed, there was someone who walked in goodness and as long as there was hope He would spare mankind.

In Genesis chapter three God tells the serpent that there is a seed coming that would crush the serpent's head. If God had destroyed mankind, those words would have been voided, and we know that heaven and earth will pass away but God's Word will never die.

God told Noah to build an **ARK**! It was going to rain! God was about to create the great escape! He was about to become Noah's "way maker." God was going to be faithful to this man, because this man had been faithful to God. Not only was God going to spare Noah, He also spared all of Noah's family. God was so merciful that He even allowed time for Noah to try to make some converts and bring others into the **ARK** with him.

Noah preached for 120 years but no one came to the **ARK** except Noah and his family. The **ARK** was a type of Christ. It was the place where you would be spared from judgment. As long as Noah stayed in the Ark he and his family would not feel the pain of judgment. Just imagine sitting in that boat and listening to all the people screaming "Noah! Let us in." All Noah could do was cling to the **ARK** (Jesus). Jesus is our **ARK**! When we come to Him and enter into His covenant, we will miss the judgment of God and be protected by the **ARK** of His blood. I believe that God will always spare our family when we, as the men of our homes, are living according to His Word and when we do, we find **FAVOR! God was Faithful to Noah and He's going to be faithful to you!**

Chapter 3
Unwavering Faith
Will Produce
The Faithfulness Of God

Heb 6:13-15
13 When God made his promise to Abraham, since there was no one greater for him to swear by, he swore by himself,
14 saying, "I will surely bless you and give you many descendants."
15 And so after waiting patiently, Abraham received what was promised. NIV

Heb 11:8-12
8 By faith Abraham, when called to go to a place he would later receive as his inheritance, obeyed and went, even though he did not know where he was going.
9 By faith he made his home in the Promised Land like a stranger in a foreign country; he lived in tents, as did Isaac and Jacob, who were heirs with him of the same promise. 10 For he was looking forward to the city with foundations, whose architect and builder is God.
11 By faith Abraham, even though he was past age-and Sarah herself was barren-was enabled to become a father because he considered him faithful who had made the promise.
12 And so from this one man, and he as good as dead, came descendants as numerous as the stars in the sky and as countless as the sand on the seashore. NIV

Heb 11:17-19
17 By faith Abraham, when God tested him, offered Isaac as a sacrifice. He who had received the promises was about to sacrifice his one and only son,
18 even though God had said to him, "It is through Isaac that your offspring will be reckoned."
19 Abraham reasoned that God could raise the dead, and figuratively speaking, he did receive Isaac back from death.
NIV

Abraham didn't just believe God in times when everything seemed to be okay or in times of great victories. Abraham believed God when everything else was failing. No matter how hard he tried, he couldn't seem to produce a child.

When God promised Abraham a son, Abraham was in his seventies. God didn't fulfill his promise to Abraham until he was almost one hundred years old. As a matter of fact, the Word of God says that God waited. God waited until Abraham was as good as dead in his natural potential to produce seed and Sarah his wife had reached the season in her life that she was unable to bear children. Why? Why did God take so long to fulfill His promise? The only answer I can offer is that we must trust God. No matter what time He chooses to fulfill His promise, He will! God will be faithful to what He has promised. Abraham believed this... He didn't allow his situation to dictate his belief system. He rested on the Words of the Lord.

> *Faith isn't faith until it passes the test of time!*

Faith isn't faith until you can pass the test of time... the test of difficulties, when there is nothing else left in human abilities. God took twenty-six years to fulfill a promise to Abraham. God waited until there was no human potential to be factored in. There was no human part in the performance... If God doesn't do it, it isn't going to get done. If God's going to be the source then you must be willing to reach the seasons of drought and emptiness. It's at the time you feel as good as dead that God will walk into your camp, home or presence and give you the very Word of encouragement that's going to bring you out and take you into your next season of promotion.

By faith when Abraham was tested and believed God, it was credited to him as righteousness. Get a good grasp of this. Good works or deeds do not obtain righteousness. That's not to say that works and deeds aren't a part of the Christian walk. The Word says that he was credited with righteousness because he took God at His Word, and nothing or no one was going to persuade Abraham otherwise.

What about Sarah? She not only required faith, she had to be the one to carry the seed of promise. Sarah had to enter a higher level of faith. Abraham believed, but Sarah not only had to believe it, she had to conceive it. The Word says that we need to have faith in our heart. There is no such thing as head faith; there is only heart faith.

There is no way you can understand how God is going to heal your cancer, or pay a bill that you have no natural funds to pay, or bring home your child who has been away from the Lord. Your mind doesn't possess that ability to understand God, but your heart does. The spirit of man has the power to believe without understanding how.

Sarah had to have the heart to conceive. There are some steps here that we need to point out for you and I to be able to walk in our promised blessing.

1. You must first believe. That's faith. Faith is now; faith is the substance of things hoped for, and the evidence of things not seen. (Heb. 11:1)

2. You must have Sarah's level of faith. You must be able to conceive it. The word conception comes from the word conceive. When the visitors came to Abraham's house one evening, they told him that Sarah would be pregnant. When Sarah heard this she laughed and the Lord asked Abraham, "Why is your wife laughing?" Sarah couldn't conceive it in her mind that she was going to be pregnant. After all, it had been twenty-six years and there still was no promised child. The Lord was going to perform the miracle, but waited another year. He had to get Sarah ready to conceive. Conception is the ability to see your promised blessing and carry it internally.

3. When you can believe it and conceive it, you will be ready to receive and achieve it.

Abraham's faith produced his son Isaac. Isaac's name means laughter. No matter how long it takes for God to produce His promise, when it comes you will be filled with so much joy and excitement that you will be laughing, shouting, and dancing. When you come out of something your praise and worship is different. I love to watch people who stay focused through their crises and then watch them praise when God's promises come to pass. Faith in God will produce the faithfulness of God.

Chapter 4
Submission to God's Instructions Will Produce The Faithfulness Of God

What is submission?

Webster defines submission as "the quality or condition of being submissive; resignation; obedience; meekness a) the act of submitting something to another for decision, consideration, etc. b) something thus submitted, as an article or photograph to a publisher c) Law an agreement whereby parties to a dispute submit the matter to arbitration and agree to be bound by the decision".

To be a submissive person you must know the one to whom you are being submissive. There must be a confidence in and a trust of what you are being asked to do. To be submissive you must come into agreement with the one who is asking of you. A spirit of meekness is applied to your heart. You may not like what you are being asked to do, but no matter what, you submit!

Christians need to learn the art of trusting God and submitting to His will and Words. We want too often to do everything our own way.

Christianity isn't an independent walk. It is a dependent walk.

God wants us to depend on Him. He wants to be our supplier. He wants us to expect Him to take care of us and not to worry about tomorrow, but trust Him for our needs today.

Abraham and Isaac were men who had learned to walk in complete submission.

The Test of all Tests!

After Isaac was born and was of a good age God came to Abraham and asked him to sacrifice his only son, Isaac, on the mountain.
Gen 22:2

2 Then God said, "Take your son, your only son, Isaac, whom you love, and go to the region of Moriah. Sacrifice him there as a burnt offering on one of the mountains I will tell you about." NIV

Imagine if you can with me. God has required back from Abraham what He so generously gave him. Again, why? Why would God put Abraham through such a painful experience? Why after giving him the gift would He ask for it back? What's wrong with Abraham? He doesn't even offer up an argument to God. What about Isaac? He just sits there and allows his father the access necessary to tie him up and put a knife to his throat. Everything in this story is so outside the norm that if we don't take the time to get in the spirit we will develop a cynical, unrealistic approach in our interpretation.

Let's first dive into the mind of Abraham and move into the

mind of God.

Abraham had been requested to sacrifice Isaac on Mount Moriah Genesis 22:2. He waited so long for the fulfillment of this promise that it is almost absurd for Abraham to even comply with God's request. Abraham has such an awesome love for God that he doesn't even offer up an argument. Isn't this the man that pleaded with God to spare Sodom and Gomorrah? He continually pleads with God in one of the greatest sales reductions. God kept dropping His number to accommodate Abraham's request. But here with his own son he doesn't even try to offer a substitute.

Gen 18:22-25
22 The men turned away and went toward Sodom, but Abraham remained standing before the LORD.
23 Then Abraham approached him and said: "Will you sweep away the righteous with the wicked?
24 What if there are fifty righteous people in the city? Will you really sweep it away and not spare the place for the sake of the fifty righteous people in it?
25 Far be it from you to do such a thing—to kill the righteous with the wicked, treating the righteous and the wicked alike. Far be it from you! Will not the Judge of all the earth do right?" NIV

What total submission to the will of God... What was the Lord really after? I believe that God wasn't really looking for a human sacrifice in killing Isaac, but a willing sacrifice totally submitted to trusting God, even to the point of surrendering what you love the most. After all isn't God going to be required to do just that for us? God won't have anybody hiding in the wings to save His sacrifice.

Can't you just picture this man packing for his journey and sitting down at the supper table the night before his departure explaining to his wife, Sarah, what the Lord has requested of them? "God wants what? He's asking you to do what? Kill the promise seed! You've got to be kidding me! We waited so long, are you sure Abraham?" "Yes," replies her husband. "So be it. Do whatever you see fit". What an awesome wife Sarah was to be willing to let go and trust her husband. Well, it's easy to trust someone if you know that they have a daily walk and relationship with God the creator. How many men do you know who cook dinner for God and God sits down to eat it?

Let's look at these passages and get an in-depth look at the scriptures.

Gen 22:3-5
3 Early the next morning Abraham got up and saddled his donkey. He took with him two of his servants and his son Isaac. When he had cut enough wood for the burnt offering, he set out for the place God had told him about.
4 On the third day Abraham looked up and saw the place in the distance.
5 He said to his servants, "Stay here with the donkey while I and the boy go over there. We will worship and then we will come back to you." NIV
What a type and shadow of God and Jesus. Notice that first Abraham had to take a journey to Mount Moriah. This is in reference to the journey the Lord Jesus had to take to be born, trained and live as a human.

Secondly, when Abraham reached his destination, it was on the third day. Three is a significant number. The number 3 in the Hebrew means power or resurrection. Thirdly, in verse 5 we see a donkey in the story. We can recall that Jesus tells his disciples to go to Jerusalem; that there will be a donkey tied up; to tell the owner that the Lord is in need of it. Jesus rode into the city riding a donkey and the people are crying out, "Hosanna". What symbolism! What foreshadowing of what God was doing in the Old Testament would actually take place 2000 years later in the New Testament. Let me emphasize here that you will never be able to understand what God wants if you ignore the power of the **Old Testament**.

There was a professor in Bible College who used to say "you will never be able to understand the New Testament unless you grasp an understanding of the Old Testament." Never let someone convince you that you are not supposed to live by or will ever need to live by the words of the Old Testament. **That's a lie!**

What was God doing? He was testing Abraham's love and commitment. After all, he was going to be the father of many nations. God knew if he weren't able to sow his seed, he would never be able to collect, or reap his harvest. The same applies for you and me. When God asks for our seed it's not the seed that He has in mind, **it's our harvest!** Abraham's words to his servants gives you a clue that he had enough faith in God that <u>they</u> would be back not just <u>him</u>.
…We will worship and then we will come back to you."

"We will go and we will return." Emphasis on the word we! Abraham was confessing his results to his servants for his obedience. He was saying, I'm going to be submissive; I'm going to sow this seed! But I'm not coming back empty handed… **WE WILL BE BACK!** If I kill him, **God will raise**

him!

Abraham had faith in God... this God that he had become familiar with. Abraham had built a trust in God, because he was a man that talked (prayed) to God often. He had possessed the mind of God and the attitude of God. He was going to be obedient to this Jehovah and trust Him in total obedience.

Abraham wasn't going to hold anything back from worshipping God. He wasn't about to do anything or allow anyone to stop him from showing God how much he loved Him.

What about you and me? What are we holding back that keeps us from walking in total obedience? What are we allowing to stay in our lives that God has been requiring us to sow? We will never possess the blessings of Abraham as long as we continue to hold on to the things that God has been requiring us to sow. God is testing us just as He did Abraham to see what we are willing to walk away from. If Abraham could not have walked away from Isaac then he would have loved Isaac more than the **Word of God**. We must love God's Word more than anything else in our lives. There is an encouraging word in this. If we love God's Word more than anything else in our lives, God is able to do the impossible. All we need to do is believe, conceive and receive!

Just let your mind wander right now and visualize this with me. Abraham was acting in blind, total submission to God in every step up his mountain of trial, every rock, boulder and weed he pulled at to take him closer to his act of submission. Don't think for one moment that Abraham wasn't fighting the same mental battle that you and I fight every time we set out to obey the Words of the Lord.

He would occasionally look over at his son, and he would begin to feel light headed as his heart began to beat with the pain of his love for him. Abraham in his mind was going through all the steps of sacrifice and crying in his heart, **"Can I do it, can I bring myself to kill what I love so much?" Do I really love God that much? Will I succeed or fail? Oh God help me! I need you in this hour of trial."** Let me interject a thought here. God never said a word after he gave Abraham the test. Why? **When the student is taking a test the teacher doesn't talk.** If the teacher has to speak during the test and explain what's going on, then you haven't really learned anything. The time to learn something in life is when you are living on top of things. When everything is going good, take the time necessary to prepare yourself for the test. Get into the Word of God and learn what the Lord needs you to learn so you can **pass the test!** When you are in a hard place and you are perplexed and are wondering why you can't hear God, just remember that maybe you are taking the test! Just hang on and pass the test. Rewards come after the test, not during.

What about Isaac? He's at an age where he can oppose Abraham. What if Abraham gets to the place and Isaac says no! I will not go through with this insane idea. When they get to the place Isaac asks daddy where the sacrifice is.

Gen 22:6-7
7 Isaac spoke up and said to his father Abraham, "Father?"

"Yes, my son?" Abraham replied.

"The fire and wood are here," Isaac said, "but where is the

lamb for the burnt offering?" NIV

Gen 22:8
8 Abraham answered, "God himself will provide the lamb for the burnt offering, my son." NIV

Even at the end of his journey Abraham is keeping the faith. "God himself will provide the lamb." Say that and hear the prophetic words in them... **"God Himself" "God Himself"** And God himself provided that day and thousands of years later the sacrifice when Jesus was placed on the cross for you and me.

Gen 22:9-14
9 When they reached the place God had told him about, Abraham built an altar there and arranged the wood on it. He bound his son Isaac and laid him on the altar, on top of the wood.
10 Then he reached out his hand and took the knife to slay his son.
11 But the angel of the LORD called out to him from heaven, "Abraham! Abraham!" "Here I am," he replied.
12 "Do not lay a hand on the boy," he said. "Do not do anything to him. Now I know that you fear God, because you have not withheld from me your son, your only son."
13 Abraham looked up and there in a thicket he saw a ram caught by its horns. He went over and took the ram and sacrificed it as a burnt offering instead of his son.
14 So Abraham called that place The LORD Will Provide. And to this day it is said, "On the mountain of the LORD it will be provided." NIV

Isaac never lifts a finger to stop his father. He lets him tie him up, he lets him put him on the wood and watches as his father draws the knife for the kill. What an obedient son. Isaac represents not only the Jesus, but he also represents you and me. He was a living sacrifice. He had to choose to let his father do what he needed to do to fulfill not Isaac's purpose but his father's purpose.

That's exactly what we do when we choose to obey the Lord's will and fulfill in our lives what the will of the Lord is. When we fulfill His purposes and not ours, we will see the **faithfulness of God** present.

Every step up that mountain of **uncertainty**, the sacrifice, the blessing… the ram was climbing at the same pace on the other side of Abraham's mountain of trial and obedience. As long as he kept climbing he was about to crash right into his provision. Let me give you the scripture that made Abraham shout out the F.O.G. God is faithful.

Gen 22:15-18
15 The angel of the LORD called to Abraham from heaven a second time
16 and said, "I swear by myself, declares the LORD, that because you have done this and have not withheld your son, your only son,
17 I will surely bless you and make your descendants as numerous as the stars in the sky and as the sand on the seashore. Your descendants will take possession of the cities of their enemies, 18 and through your offspring all nations on earth will be blessed, because you have obeyed me." NIV

Total submission to the instructions of God will produce the faithfulness of God in your life, just as it did for Abraham.

God is and will always be at the end of your submission; He will not let you perish in your submission.

If you're in a spiritual or physical struggle right now... Don't give up and don't quit; just set your face toward heaven and trust God... Who is able to get you out. I promise this, you will not come out empty handed.

Gal 6:9
9 And let us not be weary in well doing: for in due season we shall reap, if we faint not. KJV

Chapter 5
Servanthood
Will Produce
The Faithfulness Of God

Ps 35:27-28
27 The LORD be exalted, who delights in the well-being of his servant."
28 My tongue will speak of your righteousness and of your praises all day long. NIV

Ps 116:16-19
16 O LORD, truly I am your servant; I am your servant, the son of your maidservant; you have freed me from my chains.
17 I will sacrifice a thank offering to you and call on the name of the LORD.
18 I will fulfill my vows to the LORD in the presence of all his people,
19 in the courts of the house of the LORD—in your midst, O Jerusalem. Praise the LORD.   NIV

The word **"servant or bondservant"** is not a word we hear much about in our society. For us to really gain a deeper walk with God, we are going to have to bring these words back to our lifestyle. Acquiring an understanding of what it means to be a "servant or bondservant" will help us walk deeper into the F.O.G. (Faithfulness of God)

In Bible times when the master of a house or plantation would let his slave or slaves go free, whether it was for friendship or the year of Jubilee, if the slave chose to come back and stay in and under his master's care, then he wasn't just an ordinary slave he became a **"Bondservant."**

The master would take him over to the doorpost and the slave would put his ear on the door jam. The master would take a sharp object and mark the ear and put an earring in it. This would signify that he wasn't just a slave; he was a bondservant who chose to stay and serve by his own will.

The word servant appears 515 times in the Bible and in our twenty-first century we have become very uncomfortable when we hear the word servant.

Now we are all called to be servants in the house of God. To be a servant we must be willing to do what it takes to fulfill the purposes of God. Servant simply means to WORK!

Yes, you read it correctly! Work. Favor, increase, blessings, money, health and anything else that you want will only come when you work. Someone once said, "no one whose name is worth remembering, ever lived a life of ease." Nowhere in the Word do we find anything that even gives us the hint that life would be easy and would be work free. If we want to see our home, our occupation, and our church life fruitful we must bind together and serve the purposes of God, and that purpose is to build a church that will **"Make the Devil Pay!"**

I pastor a church in Hickory, North Carolina, and I can tell you that the most frustrating thing to me is when I have to beg and plead with people to work. Oh, they'll come forward to work in the **"limelight."** People will volunteer for pulpit or teaching ministries, but don't ask for help in the nursery or children's ministry. Make petitions for someone to help keep the church clean or to do maintenance and no one comes forward.

Don't misunderstand me. I'm not saying that my sheep are lazy and won't work. They'll work! At their jobs... At their homes or to make sure that everything for their personal needs are accommodated... They'll even stay up all night to make a profit. When asked, "why weren't you at church?" They stayed home to make sure the yards are manicured, cars are washed and they are rested up for the next day... And try to instruct them as their Pastor... They look at you with a smug and a self-assured look and say, **"don't preach legalism at me."** Excuse us! who care enough about church to question the attendance and attitudes of the ones God has placed us over!

Why is it that supposedly God-fearing Christians will stay home on Wednesday night to make sure their personal life is taken care of and miss the mid week service. I believe it's a shame when we run 300 on a Sunday morning and we can't even average half that in our mid week services.

Let me take it a **little bit further**... There's Monday, Tuesday, Thursday, Friday, and Saturday, yet it will be the night we have decided to have our "**Mid Week**" service for half the body to stay home. What are they doing? Cutting their lawns, taking out their children for their birthday, or taking a ride through the country. They have no sense of respect for the corporate anointing. I'm not trying to throw water on your parade, but I know that if we don't put the church back in perspective we are going to miss a revival of His Presence.

Come on church! We have to step up in our work ethics in our churches. If you are not attending a church somewhere regularly, start! Get with the program... Your Pastor needs you... He wants you to help him.

> *No Pastor Can build a Church or Ministry by himself or herself...*

No pastor can build a church by himself... They can't pay everybody. We need the sheep to start focusing on the church again. Just walk around your church and open your eyes... look and see what needs to be done and don't wait for someone to do it... you do it. You don't need a spiritual calling to clean the bathrooms or vacuum the carpet or to pick up the area around you. You don't have to wait for some divine revelation to fall from heaven. If you are looking for a Word from God, open your ears and listen. Your pastor has been speaking for God for a long time.

Don't attend everyone else's bible studies when your local church is offering one. Don't go and engage yourself in helping other churches until you are fulfilling what you're suppose to do in your church. God didn't plant you in the church down the street; He planted you in the church you are attending right now. You and I can only produce a harvest if we remain planted in the soil. If you keep trying to place and replace yourself in every other field, you will never develop good strong biblical roots. Without a good root system your harvest will never come.

SERVANTHOOD IS NOT A CUSS WORD!

"And all the pastors shouted...Amen!"

Serving and being a servant will produce the "Faithfulness of God." In the Word of God we find such a person who went beyond just what was expected of her. When she did she was the very person who was chosen to own the goods she was serving. Her name was Rebecca.

Gen 24 -4
1 Abraham was now old and well advanced in years, and the LORD had blessed him in every way.
2 He said to the chief servant in his household, the one in charge of all that he had, "Put your hand under my thigh. 3 I want you to swear by the LORD, the God of heaven and the God of earth, that you will not get a wife for my son from the daughters of the Canaanites, among whom I am living,
4 but will go to my country and my own relatives and get a wife for my son Isaac." NIV

Gen 24:10-15
10 Then the servant took ten of his master's camels and left, taking with him all kinds of good things from his master. He set out for Aram Naharaim and made his way to the town of Nahor.
11 He had the camels kneel down near the well outside the town; it was toward evening, the time the women go out to draw water.
12 Then he prayed, "O LORD, God of my master Abraham, give me success today, and show kindness to my master Abraham. 13 See, I am standing beside this spring, and the daughters of the townspeople are coming out to draw water. 14 May it be that when I say to a girl, 'Please let down your jar that I may have a drink,' and she says, 'Drink, and I'll water your camels too'—let her be the one you have chosen for your servant Isaac. By this I will know that you have

shown kindness to my master."
15 Before he had finished praying, Rebekah came out with
her jar on her shoulder. NIV

Gen 24:16
16 The girl was very beautiful, a virgin; no man had ever
lain with her. She went down to the spring, filled her jar and
came up again. NIV

Notice that Abraham took ten camels and filled them with all
kinds of blessings… Remember that Isaac is a type and shadow of Jesus and Rebekah is a type of the church. Abraham
sent ten camels full of good stuff with his servants. Who is this
stuff for? Not the servants, not for Rebekah's family. No, this
good stuff was held in reserve for the bride of Isaac… When
was the bride going to be able take her place and receive her
good stuff? When she accepts her invitation to come!

When is the church going to receive her stuff? When she is
willing to (1) accept the invitation to come to Jesus and (2)
willing to serve the purposes of the Father. (3) willing to leave
everything to follow her bridegroom (Jesus).

When the servants of Abraham reached Mesopotamia they
were tired and thirsty. They stopped by a well and noticed a
damsel. Her name was Rebekah.

The servant prayed to the Lord…

12… "O LORD, God of my master Abraham, give me suc-
cess today, and show kindness to my master Abraham. 13
See, I am standing beside this spring, and the daughters of

the townspeople are coming out to draw water. 14 May it be that when I say to a girl, 'Please let down your jar that I may have a drink,' and she says, 'Drink, and I'll water your camels too'—let her be the one you have chosen for your servant Isaac. By this I will know that you have shown kindness to my master."

Look closely at his prayer… First he prayed "Lord give me success today. We are never going to achieve and accomplish anything for God if we don't pray daily for Godly success. This prayer wasn't for them; they were on a mission for the master and in that mission they were desirous of succeeding for their master's sake. They prayed, **"Lord give us success today."** When the body of Christ becomes so driven that the only real desire in them is to fulfill the purposes of God, we will see the cloud once more in our midst.

We need to become a church again that will cater to the cloud and not the crowd.

Secondly, the servant put a test on the bride… The test was servanthood. **SERVANTHOOD!**

> **The Church needs to cater to the CLOUD and not the CROWD!**

14 May it be that when I say to a girl, 'Please let down your jar that I may have a drink,' and she says, 'Drink, and I'll water your camels too'—let her be the one you have chosen for your servant Isaac. By this I will know that you have shown kindness to my master."

This, in my opinion, wasn't a test of just doing the work; it was also a test of what kind of character (attitude) this bride would have. Think for one moment and imagine yourself having to first of all fulfill your obligation of getting water for your family because that's what you've been assigned to do as your personal responsibility. Secondly, you're asked by a total stranger to help bring some water. What would your response be? After all these strangers from a different country are not your responsibilities. Maybe you're tired and just don't want to help. Whatever your response would be, Rebekah's response passed the test.

What Rebekah does is amazing. She not only takes care of her personal responsibilities, she takes care of Abraham's servants and then, while they are drinking and resting, she offers to take care of all ten of their camels.

She is running back and forth filling the trough with buckets of water. Do you have any idea how much water a camel can drink? Camels consume a great amount of water. Rebekah had ten camels to satisfy. This woman had to carry gallons and gallons of water to the trough. Let's consider this… her act and attitude of servanthood required more from her than just a few minutes of work. She used an amazing amount of effort, time and strength… She must have been no less than exhausted.

However, imagine her as she looks over every camel and notices all the good stuff they are loaded down with. Maybe she felt the fur and silk and imagined herself in them… She saw the gold, silver and jewels and thought how beautiful they would look on her.

She never one time considered that the camels and all that

stuff she was taking care of was actually going to be hers. When we serve the purposes of God and we are willing to work to fulfill His cause, God will be faithful to us.

There is a difference between doing the work of a servant and having the attitude of a servant. One is an outward response to an external gain; the other is the fiber of what we are made of. Just doing the work of a servant will eventually frustrate you and when you are being treated like a servant you will show your true colors. There will be outbursts of rebellion and sarcasm. What you are really made of is cheap imitation. There's no real servant, just someone trying to do the work of a servant to gain access to someone or something.

Let me show you a parable in the Word that will explain this…

SERVANT WORKER VS SERVANT ATTITUDE!

There are those among us who only want to hang out with us for the promotion we can offer them. Their attitude is to use the work of a servant to gain your favor and in the process gain for themselves a position or a raise to a different level. The problem with that attitude is that it is an attitude of self-promotion and not Godly promotion.

These people will try to serve you, but… let me warn you… they are out to use you. Their heart is not the heart of a servant. They are your Judases waiting to sell you for thirty pieces of silver. Don't think they won't. **They will sell you**

out immediately for their gain.

How can we discover and identify these kinds of people? It's not as hard as you may think. Start treating those around you who say they want to serve you like a servant and then watch and listen. They will start to complain and moan and develop an attitude with you. They will begin to quote you their resume' and all they've done for you. When they begin to do that, cut them loose. They are out to self promote at the expense of you!

There's a pastor friend of mine who says, **"Immediately fire disloyalty."** When I first heard this statement I was led in my heart to feel that this was a statement made with no mercy in mind. I have since changed my mind, because you see, disloyalty is a heart problem. If you discover this attitude around those who are helping you build the Kingdom of God or even trying to help you build your business, fire them immediately. Trust me, you will thank me later. These people aren't promoting you...they are weighing you down.

The night that Jesus was to be arrested he made a statement to his disciples: "one of you will betray me tonight." The disciples looked around the table and asked... **"Is it I, Lord**?" with the exception of John who asked, **"Who is it, Lord**?" and Judas who says **nothing**. Why?

Judas knew he was the one and John never had one bad thought about Jesus. Watch out for those who are too quiet around you when you are looking for support. Silent people in my opinion are the ones you are not sure of. When you're looking for verbal support... this silent kind could very easily be your Judas. Don't take silence as a sign that they are with you… **Question them openly; make those who say nothing respond to you.** They will show their attitude when they speak. Let's look at a servant attitude.

A servant's heart is a heart to serve without looking for anything at all. They are the ones who will take care of your problems without looking for your hand or trying to gain your access. They will just do what they do because they love God and they love you and what you stand for.

My Spanish pastor, Tito Crespo, came to my church from Miami, Florida. When he came in the door he asked me "What can I do for this church?" I responded that we needed someone who would be willing to keep the bathrooms clean.

He never said anything about it, nor did I. One day I was walking by the restroom area when all of a sudden I heard someone singing and crying out loud in the men's room as I approached the door. What I heard was absolutely amazing to me. I peeked in through the door and saw a grown man crying on his hands and knees cleaning the bathroom floor. The whole time he was cleaning he was saying, **"Oh God thank you for allowing me the opportunity to serve you and clean your house. Lord I praise you and ask you to bless all those who enter these doors."** I was so moved in my heart that I thought to myself, this man is a real servant! I can tell you this, after years of ministry I have only seen a few who I could confidently say are real servants. That man was Tito Crespo!

Tito became our full time Spanish pastor a year later. No matter what goes on, to this day he is a servant. God will always find a way to promote real servants. I know that there are ten camels full of good stuff set up for Tito Crespo. I know that there's a harvest for all those who remain a servant in the body of Christ.

Ministry isn't about buildings or programs. Ministry isn't about the size of our congregation. No, ministry is about **servanthood**. Ministry is about taking care of those who are hurting, who are in need and don't know what to do. Ministry is turning to the Lord and asking Him what you can do to change someone's life.

Servanthood will produce the **faithfulness of God**. Read the whole story about Rebekah and listen to the Holy Spirit. You will be changed as I was. Serving people is not a weakness; rather, serving people is the very heart of God.

Let me offer a comment right here. Maybe you're reading this book and you have made the statement, "I have nothing to sow." Well that's not true… there will never be days in your life where you won't have something to sow. If you don't have any money, then sow your time. Be a servant and get ready for the Lord to release your camels of good "stuff". Servanthood will produce the **F.O.G**. (faithfulness of God)

Pray this prayer with me;

Lord help me to be a servant. Help me to understand that life is not about what I'm doing or me. Help me

Lord to put you in the forefront of all I do.

Lord restore to me the joy of my salvation. Real joy of the Lord is to put Jesus first, others second and you last.

Lord I ask you to forgive me for all the bad attitudes I have portrayed to my leaders. I pray right now for my pastor and all the leaders in my church. I confess increase and health to their lives. Lord I will never talk again about someone or do anything again for my selfish gain.

In Jesus Name Amen!

Chapter 6
The Right Attitude
Will Produce
The Faithfulness Of God

Eph 4:20-24
20 You, however, did not come to know Christ that way. 21 Surely you heard of him and were taught in him in accordance with the truth that is in Jesus. 22 You were taught, with regard to your former way of life, to put off your old self, which is being corrupted by its deceitful desires; 23 to be made new in the <u>attitude</u> of your minds; 24 and to put on the new self, created to be like God in true righteousness and holiness. NIV

Phil 2:5-8
...our <u>attitude</u> should be the same as that of Christ Jesus: 6 Who, being in very nature God, did not consider equality with God something to be grasped, 7 but made himself nothing, taking the very nature of a servant, being made in human likeness. 8 And being found in appearance as a man, he humbled himself and became obedient to death- even death on a cross! NIV

1 Peter 4:1
4:1 Therefore, since Christ suffered in his body, arm yourselves also with the same <u>attitude,</u> because he who has suffered in his body is done with sin. NIV

Attitude is a very important commodity if you plan on moving up to the next level of promotion. Attitude will determine what kind of atmosphere you create around you. Atmosphere will determine what seeds God will plant. Seeds are the source of what kind of harvest you will have.

Seeds guarantee that you have a future. If anyone ever says to you, "I do not know my future", tell him or her, not true. If you have sowed seed into the Kingdom of God, you are guaranteed a future.

Your attitude will be what draws people to you or drives them away from you. Haven't you ever been around someone who always has a bad attitude? Think for a moment how they made you feel when you left their presence. Their attitude created in them, what I call a "**chip on their shoulder.**" No matter what happens they always have a rotten disposition. You are not, unless you're abnormal, going to hang around these kinds of people. The one thing I can tell you is your attitude will open the doors of access or close them.

To have a great attitude you must be willing to change. Not everyone has the gift of a great attitude. I'm not convinced that there is a gift called "attitude." I believe that attitude is a conscious decision you make in your mind. To have a good attitude you must make the necessary effort to raise your attitude. Make up your mind today that you are not going to let bad circumstances influence your attitude. No matter what is happening to you, learn the secret that will propel you out of your present situation. That secret is **PRAISE GOD NO MATTER WHAT!** Praise is the power that brings God into your atmosphere... when God enters your atmosphere you will begin to worship Him. Worship is the ability to interact with God in such a way that you begin to see things the way God sees them. Now, I don't know about you! When I climb up to God's level of perspective I begin to get a whole new look at my situation. All of a sudden there's a surge of faith! Faith is reaching out into nowhere and hanging onto nothing until it turns into something.

> **Faith is being able to reach out into nowhere and hang onto nothing until it turns into something!**

The company you keep can also affect your attitude! I don't have to know much about you. All I need to do is watch and see who your close friends are. Your group of peers will make clear to me a lot about you. You will always attract like-minded people to congregate around you. If you come to my church and all of a sudden I see all the ones who like to talk about people gravitating toward you, you're probably of like character. Our behavior will be the magnet that draws our friends. So, if you can't figure out why you have all negative people hanging out around you, you might need to check and see if you're like them. (**"Birds of a feather, flock together"**)

Eph 4:20-24
23 to be made new in the <u>attitude</u> of your minds; 24 and to put on the new self, created to be like God in true righteousness and holiness. NIV
Notice, that it says to be made new in the attitude of your minds. The right attitude is a mind thing. To have a good attitude you must understand that good or bad attitudes start in the mind. What we need to do as believers is to daily renew our minds in the Word of God to create in us the mind of

Christ. *(Phil 2:5 "Let this mind be in you, which was also in Christ Jesus: KJV)* With this we will begin to arm ourselves with the weapons that will destroy anything that tries to change our attitude. Your attitude will be the catalyst that will propel you to your season of success.

There is a person in the Bible who no matter what happened to him kept his attitude in check. That man was Joseph. Because Joseph kept the right attitude he allowed God and others to discover that he could be trusted and promoted.

Just his name gives us the first hint that this person wasn't going to be ordinary by any meaning of the word.

Gen 30:22-24
22 Then God remembered Rachel; he listened to her and opened her womb. 23 She became pregnant and gave birth to a son and said, "God has taken away my disgrace." 24 She named him Joseph, and said, "May the LORD add to me another son." NIV

Joseph was a type of Christ in that he was going to take away the disgrace of his family. His father Jacob loved Joseph dearly and at an early age began to show favor for him. Joseph's brothers were jealous of him. Remember that when you start walking in favor it will make those around you jealous. His brothers plotted against Joseph and were going to kill him but they had a change of mind and sold him into slavery instead.

If God has a plan for you, and He does, the going may be tough, but no matter what happens the circumstance won't kill you. God won't allow what you're going through to kill you... God has a plan for you... God has a destiny for you to discover, just as He did for Joseph.

Joseph had a destiny and that destiny was in Egypt. God allowed the circumstances around Joseph to push him into the direction that He needed Joseph to go. When things aren't always what you want them to be… don't let your guard down and start complaining and moaning about what you're going through. Just raise the level of your faith and walk in a right attitude.

Gen 37:36
36 Meanwhile, the Midianites sold Joseph in Egypt to Potiphar, one of Pharaoh's officials, the captain of the guard. NIV

Joseph was sold to Potiphar, one of Pharaoh's officials. Imagine how Joseph must have felt. God had given him a dream and that dream was that he was going to be blessed and even his brothers would recognize him as being blessed and bow down to his favor.

Now here he is being sold to Potiphar to be his servant. God hadn't forgotten Joseph.

Gen 39:1-6
1 Now Joseph had been taken down to Egypt. Potiphar, an Egyptian who was one of Pharaoh's officials, the captain of the guard, bought him from the Ishmaelites who had taken him there.
2 The LORD was with Joseph and he prospered, and he lived in the house of his Egyptian master.
3 When his master saw that the LORD was with him and

that the LORD gave him success in everything he did,
4 Joseph found favor in his eyes and became his attendant.
Potiphar put him in charge of his household, and he entrust-
ed to his care everything he owned.
5 From the time he put him in charge of his household and
of all that he owned, the LORD blessed the household of the
Egyptian because of Joseph. The blessing of the LORD was
on everything Potiphar had, both in the house and in the
field.
6 So he left in Joseph's care everything he had; with Joseph
in charge, he did not concern himself with anything except
the food he ate. NIV

Focus with me on the key verses of these pages verses 3 and
4.

3 When his master saw that the LORD was with him and
that the LORD gave him success in everything he did, 4
Joseph found favor in his eyes and became his attendant.
Potiphar put him in charge of his household, and he entrust-
ed to his care...

Here Joseph is a servant. His own family put him in this crisis and now he lives in a strange country about which he has
no idea or knowledge. He's around strangers and living with a
family who has been trained to serve other gods. Talk about
problems... what a mess!

Joseph had something working for him... **his attitude!**
Joseph's attitude was never damaged by his circumstances or
by what others, who betrayed him and almost killed him, had
done to him. Not one thing that happened to him could rob
him of his internal peace. He had what I call inner faith in

God and also in himself. He possessed a confidence that said to those around him, "I can make it no matter what."

Potiphar noticed it. The word says that the master saw that the Lord was with Joseph. Now Potiphar didn't discover this attribute the first time he saw Joseph. Joseph had to show the master that he was a man of integrity… he was a man who had character… he was a man of morals and he was also a religious man.

In the course of time, the master took notice that the Lord was with Joseph and the Lord gave him success in all his transactions. Joseph found favor in the eyes of his master. What promoted Joseph? You might say that it was all God's doing. I would disagree! God had a plan, but Joseph had to submit to the plan by **keeping his attitude in check**. He had to be a man who could perform in the hour of trial, and he did! Joseph found favor or grace in the time of need. His attitude got him promoted. His attitude produced the F.O.G. (Faithfulness of God.)

ATTITUDE GIVES CLARITY OF MIND!

Don't make the mistake of thinking that when everything seems to be going well you are in your field of dreams. Sometimes God gives us (rest stops) along the way. Potiphar's house was a place for Joseph to learn the ways of the Egyptians. It was a (rest stop) for Joseph to gain some strength and understanding of his surroundings. Potiphar's house wasn't God's final destination. God had a bigger picture in mind than Joseph just running Potiphar's affairs. God was after

Pharaoh and He was going to use Joseph to bless the children of Israel.

When you are walking in the proper attitude, your mind will be clear of all the "stuff" you aren't complaining about and leaking about. Your mind will be completely alert to what God is doing and the blessings that you do have. Then when the enemy comes to test you, you will be ready to run. This very thing happened to Joseph. In comes the enemy to destroy the integrity of Joseph.

Gen 39:6-8
6 Now Joseph was well-built and handsome,
7 and after a while his master's wife took notice of Joseph and said, "Come to bed with me!"
8 But he refused.

Gen 39:9-12
9 My master has withheld nothing from me except you, because you are his wife. How then could I do such a wicked thing and sin against God?"
10 And though she spoke to Joseph day after day, he refused to go to bed with her or even be with her.
11 One day he went into the house to attend to his duties, and none of the household servants was inside.
12 She caught him by his cloak and said, "Come to bed with me!" But he left his cloak in her hand and ran out of the house. NIV

Joseph was a good-looking man and Potiphar's wife desired him and set out to have him. She tried time after time to get this man to fall into her trap. Joseph's attitude was set so high that he responds to Potiphar's wife with these words: "I have been given charge over everything in my master's house and he has held nothing from me except you his wife. How can I do this against my master!" Joseph, in such a fit of character runs from her grip and in the process leaves his cloak. What Joseph was saying was, "You can have my cloak, but you can't have my character."

You may be thinking, "That's great. God is going to honor him for standing in truth and everything is going to be great." NOT YET! But hang on.

Gen 39:13-20
13 When she saw that he had left his cloak in her hand and had run out of the house,
14 she called her household servants. "Look," she said to them, "this Hebrew has been brought to us to make sport of us! He came in here to sleep with me, but I screamed.
15 When he heard me scream for help, he left his cloak beside me and ran out of the house."
16 She kept his cloak beside her until his master came home.
17 Then she told him this story: "That Hebrew slave you brought us came to me to make sport of me.
18 But as soon as I screamed for help, he left his cloak beside me and ran out of the house."
19 When his master heard the story his wife told him, say-ing, "This is how your slave treated me," he burned with anger.
20 Joseph's master took him and put him in prison, the place where the king's prisoners were confined. NIV

This woman was wicked. She falsely accuses Joseph of attacking her and her husband believed her. Potiphar's anger burned and he put Joseph into prison. Not just any prison; no, the prison he took Joseph to was the prison where the king put his prisoners. If you were going to be sent to prison this would be the one to go to, to be able to get to the King.

Look at Webster's meaning of the word attitude.

ATTITUDE:

1. The position or posture assumed by the body in connection with an action, feeling, mood, etc.
2. A manner of acting, feeling, or thinking that shows
3. One's disposition, opinion, etc.
4. One's disposition, opinion, mental set, etc.

Joseph was falsely accused and thrown into prison, but that doesn't change his posture or actions. He keeps his way of thinking and shows that no matter what happens to him he will keep a good disposition. No wonder he was so favored by the Lord. Nothing seemed to move this man into depression, not circumstances, not the enemy and not even being falsely accused. No matter what, he stays clear in thought and actions!

When our attitude is in check and we are not focusing on all the bad that's going on around us, we will have the ability to better discover the enemy. Joseph was able to keep his wits about what was going on with Potiphar's wife. He kept enough sense to run when in that kind of situation.

Now he's in jail for something he did not do. Is Joseph going to throw up his hands and give up? Is he going to lie down and say, "I've had enough?" Is he going to sit in his cell and cry about how pure he's been and how loyal he was to the Lord and to his master Potiphar? Will he begin the attitude that so many possess when nothing seems to go right, and start boasting and saying, "**look at all I've given up and done for the Lord and this is how I am repaid.**" No, Joseph is going to make good of a bad situation. Real winners never lose!

Gen 39:20-23
20 But while Joseph was there in the prison,
21 the LORD was with him; he showed him kindness and granted him favor in the eyes of the prison warden.
22 So the warden put Joseph in charge of all those held in the prison,
and he was made responsible for all that was done there.
23 The warden paid no attention to anything under Joseph's care, because the LORD was with Joseph and gave him success in whatever he did.

> *Real Winners Never Really lose!*

Once again Joseph didn't just show up and the warden put him in charge. In the course of time… Joseph had to show the warden something. He showed him through his attitude that the Lord was with him; that the Lord had showed kindness to him and that Joseph walks in the F.O.G. (favor of God).

What the devil assumed was Joseph's demise… actually propelled Joseph into his next season of promotion. Satan always makes the mistake of assuming that what was supposed to kill you, will. So Satan leaves you for dead. Psalm 119 was written for Joseph and anyone who has been where Joseph is. "**You shall not die but live and declare the works of the Lord.**" God always shows his mighty hand when we keep our faith in tact and our attitude in check. God works all things to our good according to His purpose. Joseph has once more unlocked the favor of God. *(Romans 8)*

God is about to orchestrate another level of His plan; He is about to move the right people into Joseph's life. (Access!) Sometimes the wrong place can become the right place to gain access. What seems to be the wrong place could actually become the only place to find promotion. You wouldn't perceive that prison would be a place where you could find promotion… with God all things are possible. Never allow your situation or circumstances to dictate your future. What should have killed you… what should have destroyed you will be what God uses to push you forward to take your place and collect your harvest.

Gen 40:2-4
2 Pharaoh was angry with his two officials, the chief cupbearer and the chief baker,
3 and put them in custody in the house of the captain of the guard, in the same prison where Joseph was confined.
4 The captain of the guard assigned them to Joseph, and he attended them. NIV

Joseph ministers to these men and in return asks them to remember him. Now to take a long story and shorten it, let me paraphrase the rest of the story.

Joseph interprets their dreams- the butler was restored and went back to work in Pharaoh's palace. The butler didn't forget about Joseph. Two years had passed and the butler saw one day that the king was upset and perplexed. So the butler remembered Joseph and told the king that there was a man in his prison that could interpret dreams. Pharaoh sends for Joseph.

Gen 41:14-16
14 So Pharaoh sent for Joseph, and he was quickly brought from the dungeon. When he had shaved and changed his clothes, he came before Pharaoh.
15 Pharaoh said to Joseph, "I had a dream, and no one can interpret it. But I have heard it said of you that when you hear a dream you can interpret it."
16 "I cannot do it," Joseph replied to Pharaoh, "but God will give Pharaoh the answer he desires."
NIV

Gen 41:25-27
25 Then Joseph said to Pharaoh, "The dreams of Pharaoh are one and the same. God has revealed to Pharaoh what he is about to do.
26 The seven good cows are seven years, and the seven good heads of grain are seven years; it is one and the same dream.
27 The seven lean, ugly cows that came up afterward are seven years, and so are the seven worthless heads of grain scorched by the east wind: They are seven years of famine.
NIV

Gen 41:39-45
39 Then Pharaoh said to Joseph, "Since God has made all this known to you, there is no one so discerning and wise as you.
40 You shall be in charge of my palace, and all my people are to submit to your orders. Only with respect to the throne will I be greater than you."
41 So Pharaoh said to Joseph, "I hereby put you in charge of the whole land of Egypt."
42 Then Pharaoh took his signet ring from his finger and

put it on Joseph's finger. He dressed him in robes of fine linen and put a gold chain around his neck.
43 He had him ride in a chariot as his second-in-command, and men shouted before him, "Make way!" Thus he put him in charge of the whole land of Egypt.
44 Then Pharaoh said to Joseph, "I am Pharaoh, but without your word no one will lift hand or foot in all Egypt." NIV

Joseph, because of a good attitude and faith in a good God, went from the prison to the palace. In just twenty-four hours he had a change of address.

Hang on to your faith and keep your attitude in check. Your attitude will produce the F.O.G. Faithfulness of God. You are about twenty-four hours from an address change from poverty to prosperity, from sickness to health, from worry to worship, from death to life, from divorce to a good marriage. In just twenty-four hours your whole life could change. Just keep the faith and hang on. **GOD IS AND WILL BE FAITHFUL!**

Chapter 7
Waiting on Godly Promotion
Will Produce
The Faithfulness Of God

When we begin to discern about the people who enter our atmosphere we will better equip ourselves to protect our interests.

I believe that one of the reasons for church splits and ministry wars is because we allow people with the wrong attitude to help. You may think that they would never try to self-promote, but unfortunately they do!

I will never as a Senior Pastor put a person in a position just to fill a void or to have someone work in an area in which he or she is not completely qualified and gifted to take it all the way to the highest level. When a church is trying to make a mark in the Kingdom of God and has limited finances... limited resources and limited people to choose from we tend to just let anyone fill a position. When someone comes to us expressing a desire to help, there is a surge of excitement, because we need workers. **Caution:** if we don't qualify them, our excitement will quickly turn into exasperation. Let me give you a great statement. **"IF YOU CAN'T BE COR-RECTED, YOU CAN'T BE CONNECTED."**

Those who can't and won't let you correct them have a

Jezebel spirit in them. This Jezebel spirit is what causes them to not be able to submit to Godly leadership. Jezebel is a controlling spirit and that spirit is out to do one thing; destroy the works of a man of God. Jezebel will go around your congregation and work all those who are dissatisfied with your leadership. When you're a leader, there is no way that everyone will at all times be completely for you. Those people who have a rift with their leaders would probably get over their feelings and disgruntled attitude. But then here comes Jezebel the controlling spirit, to hook up with their hurts and before long convinces them to overthrow the leadership with rebellion. Now the Word of God says that rebellion is a form of witchcraft.

How do we deal with Jezebel? We destroy her! You can't make peace with this spirit. You will not be able to contain it or control it. Don't think for one moment that you can ignore it and it will disappear. The only course of action is to immediately go after Jezebel and cut her head off! Destroy it! By the power of the Word of God raise your sword and strike the head of Jezebel. Dethrone her fast and hard. Make no treaty with this spirit. It will destroy you if you don't destroy it.

Whatever promotes you will have to sustain you. If self is promoting someone then self will have to be the power that will sustain him or her. If man is promoting you, then men will have to sustain you. Whatever is promoting you will have to have the power within it to hold you up in hard times and in difficult times. Man will fail you, self will fail you… but God will not! If God is promoting you then it will be God who holds you up and keeps your head above the cloud of despair and anguish.

Those who are seeking leadership for the sole purpose of being promoted to a certain position will never make it. Time is the dynamic and God is the promoter, if the person looking for leadership isn't willing to wait for the proper

> ### *If You Can't Be Corrected You Can't Be Connected!*

time they will become your problem. So watch those who complain about how long it's taken for them to receive their promotion. Guard yourself from people who are only interested in a position or promotion. When you find those who are willing to wait on God, they are the ones you want to surround yourself with. When you find a person who only talks about when, where and why they haven't been used or asks why others are being used more than them…those are the very ones who are self-promoting. They are the Judases that will betray you for their own selfish promotion.

Men or women who are willing to wait on Godly promotion no matter how long it takes will find the F.O.G. (faithfulness of God.)

There is a man in the Bible who shows this kind of personality. His name is Joshua!

Ex 24:13
13 Then Moses set out with Joshua his aide, and Moses went up on the mountain of God. NIV

Num 27:18-21
18 So the LORD said to Moses, "Take Joshua son of Nun, a man in whom is the spirit, and lay your hand on him.

19 Have him stand before Eleazar the priest and the entire assembly and commission him in their presence.
20 Give him some of your authority so the whole Israelite community will obey him. NIV

Notice that God appointed Joshua to be the predecessor to Moses. God commanded Moses to lay his hands on him and give him a portion of his anointing.

When we are allowing those around us to step up we must empower them to have some authority… We can only do this if we have confidence in the person we are appointing. If I as a leader am not sure that you are out for my best interest and the interest of my church, then I will be hesitant to appoint you in an assistant's role.

What does it really mean to be an assistant?

An assistant is really someone who is willing to take up the areas that you as the leader don't have time to or want to do.

If you study the relationship between Moses and Joshua you will find the word "aide" popping up often. Joshua was Moses' aide or assistant. Now Joshua was picked by God and trained by man. God will always have someone mentor you and that someone may not be the one to take you all the way, but, no matter what, you must stay in your assistant role until such time as God sees fit to promote you.

Assistant is nothing more than a servant to the leader. Webster defines the word assistant as:
    1. Assisting; helping; that serves as a helper a person who assists or serves in a subordinate position; helper 2 a thing

that aids

An assistant is someone who God has seen fit to stand beside the leader without any threat of a hostile takeover. We need to be very cautious as leaders when allowing someone this kind of access. The sin of familiarity can destroy you and your relationship with your assistant.

When we are in need of an assistant we need to wait on the Lord and allow God the time it takes to pick us a Joshua. What we tend to do as leaders is to move faster than God has planned for us to move. Don't just put people around you who you like or who desire to be around you. Find those who will add to your weakness. Only a fool believes he has no limitations! Build to your weaknesses. Understand what it takes for a team fit. When looking, make sure that the person you're looking for has your best interest in mind.

Seek the Lord and make sure that there is a team fit... that the person you are allowing access has no problem with being asked to leave the room, handle not being told everything. Make certain that the person you are allowing around you has your best interest in mind and not their promotion. A real assistant has no problem with being second, until such time as God promotes him to being number one.

When God was getting ready to give Moses the law He had Moses go up to Mount Horeb... the mountain of God. God informs Moses to come to the mountain alone and to make sure no one sees him coming...

A good assistant has to be able to let you go alone sometimes, but in your absence he is to stay focused on what you have put into the people. There are always two kinds of leaders in your camp... first there are the Aarons who are only listening to what the people want. Secondly, there are the Joshuas who, no matter what the people want, stay loyal to you.

Aaron is one of those leaders who is always lending an ear to the complaints of the crowd. This is dangerous, because when you are gone and not in front of the crowd, your leaders must stand in your place with the same convictions as you would have. Aaron leaders are the ones who listen and then reply to the crowd and give them what they want. What happens in this scenario is the one who is giving the people what they are demanding instead of following you, and your instruction undermines you, as the main leader... this will bring punishment down upon the people. Watch out for those who are always concerned with what the crowd is complaining about; they may be the very one feeding the crowd the information.

When setting up your assistant make sure they possess the ability to be a servant. The first criterion for an assistant is servanthood.

Joshua was one of those assistants willing to wait on Godly promotion. Just think for a moment how long it took for Joshua to finally take his place as the leader of the Israelites. He was one of the spies who entered the land of promise and returned with the report that they could take the land while the others were convinced that the giants were bigger and stronger than God.

He was the one who had to wait for Moses while he was spending time with God on top of the mountain. When Moses returned Joshua was waiting half way down the mountain.

He had to wander for forty years with the children of Israel and wait while God punished all those who grumbled and complained. Can you imagine what Joshua must have felt when he heard the law of God and that God was going to kill off all those who disobeyed? Talk about being patient. Most of our assistants can't wait five years, let alone forty.

Deut 1:37-40
37 Because of you the LORD became angry with me also and said, "You shall not enter it, either.
38 But your assistant, Joshua son of Nun, will enter it. Encourage him, because he will lead Israel to inherit it.
39 And the little ones that you said would be taken captive, your children who do not yet know good from bad—they will enter the land. I will give it to them and they will take possession of it.
40 But as for you, turn around and set out toward the desert along the route to the Red Sea." NIV

Joshua was not about to take his place any time sooner than when God desired him to do so. Joshua's time finally came.

Deut 34:9
9 Now Joshua son of Nun was filled with the spirit of wisdom because Moses had laid his hands on him. So the Israelites listened to him and did what the LORD had commanded Moses. NIV

Josh 1:1-5
1:1 After the death of Moses the servant of the LORD, the LORD said to Joshua son of Nun, Moses' aide:
2 "Moses my servant is dead. Now then, you and all these

people, get ready to cross the Jordan River into the land I am
about to give to them-to the Israelites.
3 I will give you every place where you set your foot, as I
promised Moses.
4 Your territory will extend from the desert to Lebanon, and
from the great river, the Euphrates-all the Hittite country-to
the Great Sea on the west.
5 No one will be able to stand up against you all the days of
your life. As I was with Moses, so I will be with you; I will
never leave you nor forsake you. NIV

When it was Joshua's turn to lead, God was with him every
step of the way. He had such power and abilities... he did
more than Moses because God was with him and because
Moses mentored him.

There's another person who waited on God and, because of
his ability to wait, God was also with him in a mighty way.
His name was David.

The power to wait is the power to achieve with less stress.
Patience is not something we do well as humans. We are not
the kind of people who know how to wait on things. There is
power in waiting.

Isa 30:18
18 Yet the LORD longs to be gracious to you; he rises to
show you compassion. For the LORD is a God of justice.
Blessed are all who wait for him! NIV

Isa 40:28-31
28 Hast thou not known? hast thou not heard, that the ever-
lasting God, the LORD, the Creator of the ends of the earth,

fainteth not, neither is weary? there is no searching of his understanding.
29 He giveth power to the faint; and to them that have no might he increaseth strength.
30 Even the youths shall faint and be weary, and the young men shall utterly fall:
31 But they that wait upon the LORD shall renew their strength; they shall mount up with wings as eagles; they shall run, and not be weary; and they shall walk, and not faint. KJV

Joshua was willing to wait… David was willing to wait for Godly timing.

Patience is the ability to wait without complaint. Webster has a great definition…

  1   the state, quality, or fact of being patient; specif., a) the will or ability to wait or endure without complaint b) steadiness, endurance, or perseverance in the performance of a task
  2 [Chiefly Brit., etc.] solitaire (sense 3)

Don't you just love this definition! Patience is the product of endurance, the ability to stand in the middle of your life and not allow things to upset you in such a way that you begin to complain about them.

I love the word "stoicism": endurance without flinching to pain or pleasure.

When we train ourselves to walk at such a level to be able to wait on Godly promotion, we begin to walk in such power and peace that it will drive the enemy crazy. The key to not failing and missing your destiny is, no matter what's happening to you, just keep on walking. When men are praising you, keep on walking… when they are talking bad about you, just keep on walking… when you're in the storm, just keep on walking.

The storm doesn't have to be moving for you to get out of it sooner… just keep walking and you will exit your storm sooner than those who decide to sit and complain about it.

Patience is waiting on God without complaint. There's no possible way you can praise God at the same time you're complaining about things. With society being so self-satisfying it's no wonder we don't hear many testimonies about how God brought people out of their crises. When we need something we can't afford we go to "rent a center." When we're sick we immediately grab a bottle of pills instead of the Word of God. We have become a generation who can't wait on anything. We are the **"microwave generation."** Talk about **revival… renewal… restoration… redemption.** What the kingdom of God needs today is a revival, renewal and restoration on the ability to wait on God.

People who can't wait will never be the ones who will build the church. They will always be the ones who bounce from ministry to ministry. They will never be satisfied and never plant themselves in one place long enough to ever experience a harvest. We as leaders need to seek the Holy Spirit for wisdom and discernment so we can discover these impatient people before they destroy all the work we've done. What has taken us years to build… they will destroy in months.

Three times God handed King Saul over to David… David

would not take the throne for himself or by his own hand. David would not touch God's anointed no matter what. David's attitude was one of character and integrity… if God wants me to be king, then God himself will have to make it happen. No wonder he was a man after God's own heart. He was willing to wait, no matter how long it took for God to promote him.

Waiting on Godly promotion will produce the F.O.G., the **faithfulness of God**. So if you've been in an area of ministry for quite some time and you're beginning to feel the strain of your service… don't complain, just raise your hands and praise the Lord… God exalts and God puts down. If you're supposed to be promoted God will open the door for you and **God will be faithful!**

Chapter 8
Faith Applied
Will Produce
The Faithfulness Of God

Satan's information is free!
God's will cost you something...
Anything worth having has a price tag
attached to it.

Faith is God's currency... If you desire anything from the Word of God to be applied to your life - healing, prosperity, victory, salvation, health and a relationship with God - you must cash in the currency of faith!

Faith is God's economics released. Faith is God's power applied to your belief system. Faith is the source that will take you into new territory without worry and fear. Faith will cause something to rise in you that will give you all the internal substance you need, so you can face the giants of life... the lions of anger... the fire of temptation. Faith is what the whole basis of heaven is built on. If you can't walk in faith you will never advance to the level of great and uncommon achievements.

To walk in faith... you must first conquer its brother. **Fear!**

Fear is the first reaction in anyone who is willing to take a chance and step out into unfamiliar places. Everyone who makes movement and decides to leave their comfort zone will have a surge of fear. Fear is our built-in warning system that says to us... this may fail and if it does what are you going to do? When fear becomes the driving force in us we turn our warning system into a power that controls us. Anything that controls us becomes what we worship and respect. When we stop making advancement because we can't control our fears, then fear has become what controls us and not faith.

Fear is a **paralyzing power**... fear can be so intimidating it can cause you to become so worried that you won't be able to do anything but sit in a room and settle for mediocrity. When Satan wants to stop what you're doing he is going to assign a **spirit of fear** to you.

> *Satan's information is free God's will cost you!*

That demon's job description is to destroy any hope of victory... to make your life a living prison and surround you in the bars of **fear, worry, stress and anxiety.**

What does it mean to be paralyzed? It's bringing into a condition a spirit of helpless inactivity... to make one ineffective or powerless.

Fear will cause you to become ineffective and powerless. Fear, if not destroyed, will stop you from giving... stop you from praising... stop you from witnessing. Fear is one spirit you better not take sitting down.

Fear was the very reason the children of Israel never entered the promised land the first time and had to wander for forty years. Fear will cause you to look at your situation and not at what God had promised.

Num 13:31-33
31 But the men that went up with him said, we are not able to go up against the people; for they are stronger than we.
32 And they brought up an evil report of the land which they had searched unto the children of Israel, saying, The land, through which we have gone to search it, is a land that eateth up the inhabitants thereof; and all the people that we saw in it are men of a great stature.
33 And there we saw the giants, the sons of Anak, which come of the giants: and we were in our own sight as grasshoppers, and so we were in their sight. KJV

What stopped them from advancing forward? It wasn't the giants or the power they were facing... the reason the children of Israel failed to advance to the next level was their mentality. They couldn't make the jump from desert living. Their views of themselves were more damaging than the enemy itself.

They couldn't shake the welfare mentality. As long as they were in the desert God fed them, clothed them and protected them. They didn't want to do anything but wander around and let something or someone else take care of them. God doesn't want lazy children. He wants those who are willing to work and fight for what they want. Trust God all the way, yes... but sit down and do nothing and wait for God to do everything, NO! To do this is welfare.

They said, "we are in our own sight as grasshoppers."
Here's a thought: when you encounter problems along the way, remember it was God who got you this far and it will be God who will carry you the rest of the way.

I've come too far to fail... I've come too far to quit... I've come too far to allow the spirit of fear to stop me.

To deal with this spirit we must create a picture in our minds that we are bigger than the problem, because God has sent us. Greater is He that is in us, than he that is in the world. We are possessing because we are possessed. **God possesses us!**

Fear lives in the crevices of the mind.

Fear will stop the faithfulness of God...

Faith is God's currency. Fear is Satan's currency. Faith is the door that holds all the blessings of God. Fear is the door that holds all the power of hell.

Fear was the door that opened the attack on Job's life.

Job 3:25
5 What I feared has come upon me; what I dreaded has happened to me. NIV

Fear did not come from God. God has not given us a spirit of fear.

2 Tim 1:7
7 For God hath not given us the spirit of fear; but of power, and of love, and of a sound mind .KJV

God did give us something. God gave us the spirit of power, and of love and a sound mind. When you are walking in faith and not fear you will always have a mind that is full of peace.

The Word says there is perfect peace whose mind is set on Jesus. God gives us perfect peace when we are focusing on Him and not our problems. To walk in power you must first walk in love. Real love produces Godly power.

1 John 4:16-18
God is love. Whoever lives in love lives in God, and God in him.
17 In this way, love is made complete among us so that we will have confidence on the Day of Judgment, because in this world we are like him.
18 There is no fear in love. But perfect love drives out fear, because fear has to do with punishment. The one who fears is not made perfect in love. NIV

I like the acronym I heard about fear.

- F. False
- E. Evidences
- A. Appearing
- R. Real

Take a moment right now and let's bind together and defeat the spirit of fear!

I agree right now with you and by the power of the Word of God we draw the sword of faith and cut off the head of the spirit of fear.

In the name of Jesus we will not walk or live in the prison of fear another day. God has not given me fear. I am a child of God and with that right comes the power to destroy all the powers of the devil. I am free today from fear.

In the name of Jesus AMEN! It's done!

This chapter was titled "faith applied." Faith alone will not produce results. Every person has been given a measure of faith.

Rom 12:3-4
...in accordance with <u>the measure of faith God has given you.</u> NIV

Rom 12:3
3 For I say, through the grace given unto me, to every man that is among you, not to think of himself more highly than he ought to think; but to think soberly, according as God hath dealt to every man the <u>measure of faith</u> KJV

God has dealt to every person a measure of faith. Faith is not something we are unfamiliar with. We operate in natural faith everyday. When you get in your car do you sit there and wonder if it will start up? No, you just turn that key with the assurance that your car will start. You had faith in the manufacturer to create a vehicle that will start.

When you go to sit down somewhere do you check the seat thoroughly and make sure that it can hold you up so you won't fall and make a fool of yourself? No, you just walk over to the seat and sit down. That took a measure of faith. You submitted to the course of believing that the chair will hold you.

If you are driving down the road and are about to go under a bridge, do you pull over and make sure the bridge is going to stand while you're underneath it? Absurd! You don't even give it one thought; you just drive right on through without a minute of worry. This also is a measure of faith. Yet bridges fall all over the world. You showed faith in the engineer… you showed faith in the contractor… you had faith in the concrete. You applied your belief system and went right on forward without hesitation.

Yet when it comes to healing, prosperity, or protection we have this inner worry that we might be missing it. We start to make up our own theology about what God meant. We rewrite our theology to accommodate our tragedies. Faith applied will produce the **faithfulness of God**. The power of heaven is to believe. Jesus said that all things are possible to him that believes. Nothing is impossible for God. God asked Jeremiah a question that fits right now. "Is there anything too hard for God?" NO!

Just believe! Faith applied, not just faith; it must be applied. To apply your faith you must first build the measure of faith you have.

Romans says that faith comes by hearing.

Rom 10:8-12
8 But what does it say? "The word is near you; it is in your mouth and in your heart," that is, the word of faith we are proclaiming:
9 That if you confess with your mouth, "Jesus is Lord," and believe in your heart that God raised him from the dead, you will be saved.
10 For it is with your heart that you believe and are justified, and it is with your mouth that you confess and are saved.

11 As the Scripture says, "Anyone who trusts in him will never be put to shame." NIV

Rom 10:14-18
14 How, then, can they call on the one they have not believed in? And how can they believe in the one of whom they have not heard? And how can they hear without someone preaching to them?
15 And how can they preach unless they are sent? As it is written, "How beautiful are the feet of those who bring good news!"
16 But not all the Israelites accepted the good news. For Isaiah says, "Lord, who has believed our message?"
17 Consequently, <u>faith comes from hearing the message,</u> and the message is heard through the word of Christ. NIV

Faith comes through hearing the Word of God. How can you hear the word? You have to speak out of your mouth what you believe. Confession is the key to applying your faith. Now hold it. If you're thinking that you can confess a new car and a new house, **you're right; you can, ON ONE CONDITION!**

That condition is that you line up with the Word of God and living according to everything the Word of God says:
-You're faithful in your tithe...
   -You're faithful in your giving...
      -You're faithful in your church attendance.
         -You harbor no ill feelings toward your
            Christian bothers and sisters in the Lord.
               -You hold your tongue and don't talk
                  about people.

Gal 4:1-3
1 What I am saying is that as long as the heir is a child, he is no different from a slave, although he owns the whole estate.
2 He is subject to guardians and trustees until the time set by his father.
3 So also, when we were children, we were in slavery under the basic principles of the world. NIV

The KJV says
Gal 4:1-4
1 Now I say, That the heir, as long as he is a child, differeth nothing from a servant, though he be lord of all;
2 But is under tutors and governors until the time appointed of the father.
3 Even so we, when we were children, were in bondage under the elements of the world:
4 But when the fulness of the time was come KJV

Faith <u>applied</u> will produce... not just faith alone. It must be applied! The level of your understanding will determine the power of your ability to apply your faith.

As long as we continue our walk as children it matters not that we have the rights of an heir to claim everything... we will not receive them. We will only receive what God believes we can handle.

We can possess enough understanding of faith to be saved... not enough to walk in healing. We can have the power to feel we are overcomers... yet never overcome. Our understanding of the Word of God is the key to everything God has set up for us through our maturity as believers. "...as long as the heir is a child, he is no different than a slave, although he owns the whole estate, he is subject to guardians and trustee…" As long as you remain as children you are in bondage and under the elements of the world.

What we have is a church full of saved heaven bound immature children who do not want to learn anything beyond salvation. Why? Because where much is given much is required. If you have been at the same spiritual level for some time, be honest with yourself. Aren't you tired of being tossed around by the enemy? Aren't you tired and fed up with having enough of God to save you from… but not enough of God to take you in?

What good is coming out of something? For example drugs, bad marital problems, hurt feelings… the list goes on and on. What good is coming out to wander like the children of Israel for forty years in the desert and never enter your next season of promotion?

In Egypt there was not enough…
> In the wilderness there was just enough…
> > In Canaan there was **MORE THAN ENOUGH!**

Faith applied is the ability to believe in what God is saying. It's the power to act on what God is saying so that you can come out of whatever you're in… Not just come out to enter your next season.

Say this out loud. I AM NOT JUST COMING OUT… I'M GOING TO ENTER MY SEASON OF BLESSINGS!

I HAVE APPLIED MY FAITH... I AM BLESSED! HEALED AND DELIVERED FROM ALL BONDAGE AND SLAVERY! I AM SO FREE. I AM SO HEALED. I WALK IN SUCH POWER AND MIGHT THAT MY MIRACLE IS RIGHT AROUND THE NEXT TURN.

MY GOD HAS NEVER FAILED... I AM NOT GOING TO FAIL EITHER. GLORY TO GOD!

We must apply our faith... we must use it daily. Faith unused becomes weak.

Read these next passages carefully...

James 2:18-26
18 But someone will say, "You have faith; I have deeds." Show me your faith without deeds, and I will show you my faith by what I do.
19 You believe that there is one God. Good! Even the demons believe that-and shudder. 20 You foolish man, do you want evidence that faith without deeds is useless?
21 Was not our ancestor Abraham considered righteous for what he did when he offered his son Isaac on the altar?
22 You see that his faith and his actions were working together, and his faith was made complete by what he did. 23 And the scripture was fulfilled that says, "Abraham believed God, and it was credited to him as righteousness," and he was called God's friend.
24 You see that a person is justified by what he does and not by faith alone.
25 In the same way, was not even Rahab the prostitute con-sidered righteous for what she did when she gave lodging to the spies and sent them off in a different direction? 26 As the

body without the spirit is dead, so faith without deeds is dead.
NIV

Notice how many times we see the word faith mixed with the word deeds. Don't misrepresent this passage. Works alone will not save you. Works alone will not move heaven. You must mix your faith with your works. You must believe, then act on what you believe. Remember, "Faith comes by hearing the Word of God." Actions come by believing what you heard.

Faith applied will produce the **faithfulness of God**. God is only going to move at the level of your faith released. Quit blaming God for things you haven't received. It's not God keeping them from you, **it's you**! God already gave you His instructions in Galatians chapter 4; if you remain as a child then you will be no different than a slave. You will be in bondage to the elements of this world.

1 Cor 13:11-12
11 When I was a child, I talked like a child, I thought like a
child, I reasoned like a child. When I became a man, I put
childish ways behind me.
12 Now we see but a poor reflection as in a mirror; then we
shall see face to face. Now I know in part; then I shall know
fully, even as I am fully known. NIV

Mature faith will take you to a place where you will be able to see and understand fully what the purpose of God is.

1 Thess 1:2-4
2 We give thanks to God always for you all, making mention
of you in our prayers;
3 Remembering without ceasing your work of faith, and

labour of love, and patience of hope in our Lord Jesus Christ, in the sight of God and our Father;
4 Knowing, brethren beloved, your election of God.KJV

This verse confirms in three words faith applied. Remembering without ceasing your work of faith... Faith is work! Whoever said faith was easy was in error. Faith is work. For faith to accomplish what God intended to accomplish it must be applied. To apply your faith is work. A better way to say this is - work your faith because faith works.

When things begin to start happening... **work your faith!**

When the enemy starts harassing... **work your faith!**

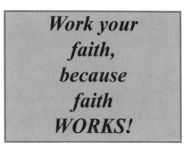

Work your faith, because faith WORKS!

When depression tries to set in... **work your faith!**

When hell is all around you and nothing seems to be working... **work your faith!**

Faith is work! Faith applied will set you up for a miracle everyday of your life.

Work your faith, **because faith works.**

Let me become a little controversial here... Sometimes no matter how much faith you have God is not going to bail you out of your problem.

God allows us to go through sufferings so that we can mature into believers who aren't moved and stirred by what's going on around them. When things that are happening to you can't break your focus, you will possess the faith that gets you through anything.

Real faith is when you're "slap dab" in the middle of the biggest crisis of your life and somehow you can still offer up praise and worship without any fear or worries about your present situation. God doesn't always want to take you out, but He always wants to help you walk through. Here's the power of faith... to hang on and allow God time to get into your pit with you. Think for a moment... if God were always bailing us out then we would never learn how to be patient.

Romans 5:1-6
1 Therefore, since we have been justified through faith, we have peace with God through our Lord Jesus Christ,
2 through whom we have gained access by faith into this grace in which we now stand. And we rejoice in the hope of the glory of God.
3 Not only so, but we also rejoice in our sufferings, because we know that suffering produces perseverance;
4 perseverance, character; and character, hope.
5 And hope does not disappoint us, because God has poured out his love into our hearts by the Holy Spirit, whom he has given us.
6 You see, at just the right time, when we were still power-less, Christ died for the ungodly. 7 Very rarely will anyone die for a righteous man, though for a good man someone might possibly dare to die. 8 But God demonstrates his own love for us in this: While we were still sinners, Christ died for us. NIV.

Our trials set us up to learn how to be mature in our walk with God. When the devil can't frustrate us through trials and tribulations; when all his efforts seem to do nothing to us because all we do is praise harder, pray harder and worship harder, we will begin to frustrate the devil.

If we want the power of Jesus we must be willing to know Him in His sufferings. The Word of God says that if we know Him in His sufferings we will share in His power of resurrection. We, through faith, can walk in the power of Jesus' resurrection. We have RESURRECTION POWER!

FAITH APPLIED WILL PRODUCE THE F.O.G.!

Chapter 9
GIVING
Will Produce
The Faithfulness Of God

I don't know what it is about money... When I start talking about money or giving, no matter how energized the service is, the whole atmosphere becomes heavy with despair and faces go from smiles to frowns, from joy to anger.

The majority of the congregation does not want to hear about giving, increase or harvest. The only explanation I can offer is this... I believe the people don't want to become accountable for what they hear. It's one thing to go around in life saved and on your way to heaven without the knowledge that you can possess a little heaven on earth through your giving.

When we hear that the law of increase and harvest only exists in the power of your seeds, we become accountable to let go of what wc have to gain what God has.

INCREASE VERSUS HARVEST!

I was in my sanctuary one day thanking God for giving me increase after I had sowed a faith seed. My wife and I sow seeds every week. We believe that instead of pleading about our financial situation we would plant.

Four years ago God changed our lives through the power of

seed sowing. We have experienced so much increase and blessings I do not have the time to testify to them all today. Here are a few!

I have been driving a C 280 Mercedes for two years and someone else is making the payment.

I'm living in a 3,000 square foot home... four bedrooms, three full size bathrooms, an office and a garage for a year now and God made the payments for the first 12 months.

My wife and I have been on two cruises to Nassau Bahamas completely paid for.

Dr. Mike Murdock took my wife and I to the Holy Land completely paid for.

I had a $6,700.00 debt hanging over my head and someone completely paid off my debt... after I had let go of a $1,250.00 seed.

Someone is always handing me cash or buying my meal or taking care of a trip. I'm so deep in the F.O.G. (favor of God) the devil can't see me.

This list could go on for pages. It all started four years ago when I began to work the power of sowing.

Not only has increase come in the way of financial favor, we have also experienced other ways of favor.

My staff at Living Word Fellowship has experienced the same F.O.G. (Favor of God)

My youth pastor has been with me since he was a teenager and is now married and working fulltime as my youth pastor. His wife is our praise and worship leader. He experienced uncommon favor! Every year we have a youth camp called **BEACH INVASION**, which I started in 1993. Each year we take 100 to 150 youth to Panama City, Florida, and turn them on to the Holy Ghost. The whole purpose for this camp is to give youth an experience with the supernatural power of God and not just religion. Our motto has always been every youth goes; money is no object. With this commitment we have had to walk in faith every year. This year we had many youth go who could not afford to pay, but we stayed true to our commitment that everyone goes. Money should never be the reason we don't minister to someone. God will take care of those who are willing to minister no matter the cost.

When camp was all said and done… we found ourselves in a deficit of $3,750.00. Now with this in mind our Children's ministry was about to have their annual KIDS CAMP 2001 in two weeks. The money for that trip was holding the ministry account up.

Both my youth pastor and children's pastor sat in my office asking me… "Pastor, what are we going to do?" TRUST GOD!

Three days later, we were at a restaurant after our mid week service… let me just say, God really moved that night in our service and we were all charged up. I'm not going to only praise God after He demonstrates His favor… no way! I'm going to praise Him beforehand.

Someone walked up to my Youth pastor and said, "We've been holding this check for a month and we want to sow this into your youth ministry." The check was for **$20,000.00** **YOU READ THAT RIGHT!**

GET READY! FOR THIS IS ONLY INCREASE... WAIT TILL OUR HARVEST SHOWS UP!

By the way, if you desire to send your youth to a radical youth camp and want more information on **BEACH INVA-SION**...call us at (828) 325-4773 or write Mindset Youth Ministries P.O. Box 3707 Hickory, NC. 28603

Our Church Administrator received a Sedan Deville Cadillac completely paid for.

Get ready for your harvest to show up! Don't let religion and stinking thinking rob you of what's rightfully yours by spiritual birth. If you're not already paying your tithe and sowing seeds, start this week. Never enter your church service without your seed to sow. I preach and teach my people at LWF... never enter the presence of God without your offering.

Everybody is getting excited about increase... but what about harvest? I was walking around my yard one day praising God about my increase and all the things God has done for me... all of a sudden I felt a quickening in my spirit. The Lord spoke to my heart and said you're getting excited about your increase... increase is not your harvest. When you sow a $100.00 and receive a $1,000.00 for sowing, that's not your harvest, it's your increase. Harvest is much greater than increase. Increase is when we gain enough to feel relief for the moment. Harvest is so much bigger.

When Harvest comes you must be able to eat from it, sow from it, save from it, take care of the needy from it. Harvest is much greater than just increase. I'm expecting harvest to come! My harvest and your harvest is a result of our giving… Whatever the enemy tries to do to you, don't let him stop your planting.

Giving will produce the **F.O.G. (Faithfulness of God)**

Gen 26:1-6
1 Now there was a famine in the land—besides the earlier famine of Abraham's time—and Isaac went to Abimelech king of the Philistines in Gerar.
2 The LORD appeared to Isaac and said, "Do not go down to Egypt; live in the land where I tell you to live.
3 Stay in this land for a while, and I will be with you and will bless you. For to you and your descendants I will give all these lands and will confirm the oath I swore to your father Abraham.
4 I will make your descendants as numerous as the stars in the sky and will give them all these lands, and through your offspring all nations on earth will be blessed,
5 because Abraham obeyed me and kept my requirements, my commands, my decrees and my laws."
6 So Isaac stayed in Gerar. NIV

Gen 26:12-15
12 Isaac planted crops in that land and the same year reaped a hundredfold, because the LORD blessed him.
13 The man became rich, and his wealth continued to grow until he became very wealthy.

14 <u>He had so many flocks and herds and servants that the Philistines envied him.</u> NIV

Notice that Isaac planted while there was a double famine in the land… In that same year he reaped a hundredfold, because the Lord blessed him. I like this, the man became rich, and his wealth continued to grow until he became VERY WEALTHY!

Wealthy is when you can keep what you have without doing what you did to get it. Riches is what you have; wealth is what your are.

Harvest is what the church needs to be seeking, not just increase. Even Jesus said to pray to the Lord of the harvest… not to the Lord of increase. Giving with the expectancy of harvest is much more focused on others than just increase. Increase is just enough to feel a present lifting of my load. Harvest will not only lift my load but those around me.

We must learn to let go of what is in our hands. We must understand that there is nothing we have that God didn't give to us. If He wanted it He could take it. He's asking us to be givers so that we won't let what we have own us… we own what we have.

> *Love people use things, don't love things and use people*

Too many Christians are in love with things. Things become our idol when we focus on them and not God. God wants us to love people and use things. Instead, we love things and use people.

We wonder why there are not a lot of things in the body of Christ. We can't handle them! God is a God of provision. The first miracle and last miracle of Elijah was provisional. The first and last miracle of Elisha was provisional and the first and last miracle of Jesus was provisional. The whole purpose of God sending His son, Jesus, was to provide for us. God is into our harvest. He wants us blessed to be a blessing. Giving is the key to harvest… Sowing is the tool.   Seeds aren't just limited to money… a smile, a kind gesture, a welcomed hand-shake are all seeds.

Sow love; reap love!
Sow kindness; reap kindness!
Sow help; reap help!

SOW MONEY… REAP MONEY!

Luke 6:38
38 Give, and it will be given to you. A good measure, pressed down, shaken together and running over, will be poured into your lap. For with the measure you use, it will be measured to you." NIV.

Notice "**IT WILL**" be given to you. What will? Whatever you have given will come back to you, pressed down and running over.

The faithfulness of God is hinged on so many aspects of our walk with God. We must learn to understand that there will never be a day in our lives when we can say, "**I have arrived.**" We are all in spiritual process, being changed from glory to glory. Giving is one area that is overlooked in the body of Christ. Satan wants to keep us broke, busted and poor.

As long as we can't pay our own bills, we will never be able to afford to take the gospel beyond our own bondage. Let us become financially liberated and we will affect the whole city, state and nation with our wealth.

LEARN TO LET GO AND LET GOD!

When I speak about giving, I don't mean our tithe. Tithe is not a giving, tithe is not seed… tithe is a **payment**. We are commanded by the Lord to pay our tithe. A tithe is 10 percent of what comes to your hand. There seems to be a lot of misunderstanding in the body of Christ about paying tithe. For some reason believers have watered down the responsibility of paying their tithe.

When we learn the biblical principles of tithing and giving we will break out into so much abundance that others would be taken care of by our abundance.

Jesus came to change our season! Before Jesus entered my life I was living in the season of drought and despair. When I accepted Him as Lord and Savior my whole outlook on life changed. Jesus took me from shallow waters to deep waters. Would you love to walk out of shallow water living? Do you desire to allow God to change your season and for you to live a life with no more dry seasons? If you desire to see and experience the **F.O.G. (faithfulness of God)** learn to tithe, sow, and be completely obedient to the Word of God.

When we give what we have to support the kingdom of God we will become blessed!

In Luke 5 we see exactly what I'm writing about take place.

Luke 5:1-9
1 And it came to pass, that, as the people pressed upon him to hear the word of God, he stood by the lake of Gennesaret,
2 And saw two ships standing by the lake: but the fishermen were gone out of them, and were washing their nets.
3 And he entered into one of the ships, which was Simon's, and prayed him that he would thrust out a little from the land. And he sat down, and taught the people out of the ship.
4 Now when he had left speaking, he said unto Simon, Launch out into the deep, and let down your nets for a draught.
5 And Simon answering said unto him, Master, we have toiled all the night, and have taken nothing: nevertheless at thy word I will let down the net.
6 And when they had this done, they enclosed a great multitude of fishes: and their net brake.
7 And they beckoned unto their partners, which were in the other ship, that they should come and help them. And they came, and filled both the ships, so that they began to sink.
8 When Simon Peter saw it, he fell down at Jesus' knees, saying, Depart from me; for I am a sinful man, O Lord.
9 For he was astonished, and all that were with him, at the draught of the fishes, which they had taken: KJV

Simon was asked from the Lord to use his ship so that He could teach the people about the kingdom. Peter had toiled all night fishing; now fishing isn't an easy job. He must have been exhausted... all night working a physical job, pulling and casting nets and then come home with no rewards for his hard work. **What a day this day is becoming...** after all this work, Jesus is requiring the assistance of his ship and with that assistance, comes more hours of no sleep... Peter has to sit on the ship and listen to the preaching of the long-winded man of God.

Jesus finishes His teaching and looks down at Simon and says, **"Launch out into the deep, and let down your nets for a draught."** The Amplified **"When He had stopped speaking, He said to Simon (Peter) Put out into the deep (water), and lower your nets for a haul."**

The Lord was changing Simon's season from shallow fishing to deep-water fishing. Imagine what was going through the mind of Simon... This man is a teacher; he was raised a carpenter and he's going to instruct me on how to fish. Doesn't Jesus realize that I have stayed up all night fishing... my nets are already clean and put up for the day... my family is already expecting me to be home? He wants me to go out into deeper waters and lower my nets. I can't believe this! Oh yes, that's right... God was about to change his season and change requires something on His part.

Watch what Simon says next! **"Master, we have toiled all the night, and have taken nothing: nevertheless at thy word I will let down the net."**

Nevertheless at thy word I will let down my net.

Amplified says "...**But on the ground of your word, I will lower my nets (again).**

Peter (or Simon), wasn't letting down his net because he wanted to...

He wasn't letting down his nets because he believed he was

going to catch anything.

He wasn't even doing it because he had faith and expectation of a blessing… No, Simon says, "On your word alone am I going to obey. Because of who you are. My obedience is not on what I'm feeling, but on what you're saying, Lord!"

When Peter obeyed… the blessing came.

"6 And when they had this done, they enclosed a great multitude of fishes: and their net brake.
7 And they beckoned unto their partners, which were in the other ship, that they should come and help them. And they came, and filled both the ships, so that they began to sink."

There was so much of a blessing that Simon had to call his partner. There was so much that the catch almost sank both their ships. Simon gave his ship and his time for the man of God to use. When Jesus was done with kingdom business He blessed the **man who gave!** God is faithful to those who learn the power of giving, or better sowing, seed. One more thing! Peter also fell down to his knees and repented and accepted the man of God and was chosen at that time to be one of His disciples. Secondly, it's only at the end of your obedience that you will discover your miracle.

> ## *AT THE END OF YOUR OBEDIENCE IS GOD'S FAVOR!*

Favor always follows obedience. When favor comes to you it will come after you have proven your obedience to God's word. If you divide the word obedience into three parts the middle word would be "die".

(OBE – DIE – ENCE) To be completely an obedient believer you must be willing to die to your flesh. The more flesh you kill, the more obedient you will become. Obedience is the qualifier to favor and to God's faithfulness. To be a good giver you must be an obedient giver.

Giving will produce the F.O.G.
(The faithfulness God)

Chapter 10
Conquering Debt
Will Produce
The Faithfulness Of God

Conquering debt will produce the F.O.G.

You aren't truly free until you are debt free... Giving is the best way to increase your storehouse. Let me mentor here. You can't just be a good giver in your church and not pay your bills at home.

The worst thing a believer can do is to lag behind on his bills. We all have times of famine and have sown in times of lack. Usually that shouldn't be the norm... if you are sowing what you owe to others, don't! Pay your bills first and be faithful to give what you have to the kingdom of God. Don't sow what belongs to others. Sow what belongs to you. Now, this isn't a popular thing to say but I believe that when you get your life in order your finances will begin to turn around... you may start out small but you will finish up big!

For example; let's say that your power bill is $150.00 and all you have in your checking account is $200.00... don't sow over what it will cost you to pay your power bill unless you are absolutely sure you have heard from God. If God is prompting you to sow at that level of sacrifice then you will have the money to pay your power bill by the due date.

Let me impress a caution. Be very careful not to let someone stir you up and in the process, forget your responsibility to your own commitments. I do not believe that God would impress on you to sow if it would cost your own reputation to be stained.

Don't misunderstand me; **I'm not saying not to sow**... I'm saying know how and when to sow. Learn to sow continuously... sow often... sow every time you're in an anointed service. Just learn to sow at your level and not at the level of others. If we would learn to sow at our level we would have abundance in our churches. However, the norm is that half of the church sows and the other half or more are freeloaders.

Five years ago my wife and I started learning the principle of prosperity and that being blessed is to be a blessing. We started sowing seeds weekly in our church. At that time we were under a lot of debt, so the amount we sowed was a whopping $10.00 a week. At that season of our lives $10.00 was a sacrifice. Now we sow $50.00 a week or more above our tithes. We can't wait until we are sowing $100.00, then $500.00 and so on weekly.

Learn to sow something! If all you have is a $1.00 sow it! It would do more for you in the soil of your faith than in your pocket.

Don't over do it, but don't under do it. Learn to stretch yourself but also make sure your bills are being paid on time. When we put money in order... we won't have to work for money; money will work for us. Money is a tool and tools are supposed to be used. When a tool breaks we get another one. Money was preordained to be used not worshipped! Money was to take care of our needs, not to be sought after 40, 50 hours a week. LET'S SHOUT IT RIGHT NOW… **"MONEY COMETH TO MY HOUSE! I WILL GET MY FINANCES IN ORDER."**

God loves when we are trying to get our house in order. He is very attentive to our desire to better ourselves and is pleased when we make the necessary efforts to do so. God will get involved with those who desire change. One of the largest setbacks in the body of Christ is **bad credit** and **slow bill payers.** My administrator told me that when he was in the financing business every so-called Christian that borrowed money from his company… never paid it back or filed bankruptcy. That is disastrous to the reputation of God and us.

Let's change this stigma that is on believers by starting today with a heart of repentance. Our character and integrity are on the line. If you can't buy it, don't charge it for the minimum payments of $10.00 a month for the next 10 to 20 years on a high interest rate. That is illogical. Wait until you have the funds for what you want and learn to trust God.

Debt is a curse and we must break it. The line is drawn here today as you're reading this book and desire to produce the **F.O.G. (faithfulness of God).** Stop the insanity of debt! Start today; make a budget and stick to it. Start paying off those high percentage credit cards and loans. I assure you that if you start this you will see God's participation in your life, finances and family. Money will start showing up un- expectantly at your dwelling. When God sees that you desire to become debt free… when He can trust that you are seeking to free up others with your freedom, He will begin to pour out His power and wisdom.

Let me give you a financial priority list
1. TITHE
2. SOW
3. BILLS
4. SAVINGS
5. YOURSELF
6. OTHERS
7. RETIREMENT OR INVESTMENTS

You cannot and will not have financial power until you are **debt free**. How can we help others if we are barely getting by ourselves?

Conquering debt will produce the **F.O.G.**

Unfortunately, this is not an exhaustive study on finances. If you really desire to change your financial future then take the time to study what financial leaders are saying. Go to your local bookstore and inquire about books on budgets, investments, good stewardship and others alike...

We can't change just because we have the desire to... we must take the necessary efforts required to change.

Chapter 11
The Right Kind of Praise Will Produce The Faithfulness Of God

The reason I phrased this chapter the "right kind of praise" because any "old praise" wouldn't produce the faithfulness of God.

One of the greatest truths believers can learn is to be of good cheer… to maintain a spirit of joy and walk in the attitude of praise in the center of troubles.

There is a doctrine going through the church arena that claims that if you can find, gain or learn how to walk in the right kind of faith we will never have to suffer or go through trials. NOT TRUE!

The truth is that the more understanding of faith you walk in, the more you and I will be tested for that understanding.

John 16:33
33 These things I have spoken unto you, that in me ye might have peace. In the world ye shall have tribulation: but be of good cheer; I have overcome the world. KJV

Jesus is speaking to His disciples these things that in me you might have PEACE. In the world you shall have tribulation.

What things?

Shall is an important word, "Shall" states in the text that we will most certainly have trials or tribulations. There's no scripture taken in its context that even hints that we would never suffer. If we plan on living a long life we better become confident that we will have to go through heartaches and trials.

The text uses the word tribulation… the Greek meaning to this word "pressure, a worn track or rut, and corrosion." As long as there is breath in your body you will have to live through some sort of heartaches. Paul made a statement that if you want to know Jesus in the power of His resurrection… you have to be willing to fellowship with him in his sufferings.

Phil 3:10
10 That I may know him, and the power of his resurrection, and the fellowship of his sufferings, being made conformable unto his death; KJV

The good news is that we do have a pattern given to us through the Word of God that if we do suffer we will somehow make it through.

Praise is the power of faith in you, it allows you to lift up your hands in the time of crises… raises your voice in the spirit of boldness and shouts that God is able. That no matter what you're in God has the ability to get you through it… unstained… undamaged and unmoved!

Jesus said, "be of good cheer." The Greek meanings to this phrase was to be bold, to be courageous, to exercise your courage in times of troubles. How can we exercise something without an opposite force going against what we are trying to strengthen? You can't! Opposition in life is nothing more than what the weights of a natural gym are to the physical body: will cause your faith and praise to develop the spiritual muscles necessary to take you to the next level of promotion and victory. The more you can lift up in your praise the more you can move with your faith. Praise will get God in your sufferings with you and where the spirit of the Lord is there is freedom and victory.

What got Paul and Silas through the beating and jail time? Praise did!

What kept Stephen in Acts from seeing his accusers? **Praise did!**

What allowed David the access necessary to be King? **Praise!**

David was a man after God's own heart. What did David possess that Saul didn't? David had a spirit of praise in him at all times. He had no problem lifting up his voice and shouting who and what His God could do. David wrote Psalms 150: **"… let everything that has breath praise the Lord…"**

My God! Wasn't it David who stripped down to his undergarments and danced all the way to the top of the mountain where the resting place of the Ark of the Covenant was to be? Praise kept the **F.O.G. (faithfulness of God)** in David's life! Others would have been destroyed for the acts of sin David committed but God kept His judgment of death away from him because David's heart was always after God.

Think for a moment about the church you attend. Does it have an attitude of Praise and Worship? I'm not talking about singing two songs and sitting down. I'm talking about a spirit and attitude of excitement and expectancy! If your pastor tried to stop it he couldn't. Praise will develop an attitude of expectancy in the house. Expectancy is the breeding ground for miracles.

Lately God has really poured into my spirit that if we don't as a people learn what real worship and praise is all about we will continue to miss the mark of what God wants for our lives.

Let me give you an acronym that will help me relate what praise will do for us.

P - IN PRAISE STANDS FOR **PUSHING BACK THE ENEMY...**

Ps 8:2
2 From the lips of children and infants you have ordained praise because of your enemies, to silence the foe and the avenger. NIV

Ps 9:2-6
2 I will be glad and rejoice in you; I will sing praise to your name, O Most High.
3 My enemies turn back; they stumble and perish before you.
4 For you have upheld my right and my cause; you have sat on your throne, judging righteously.
5 You have rebuked the nations and destroyed the wicked; you have blotted out their name forever and ever.
6 Endless ruin has overtaken the enemy, you have uprooted

their cities; even the memory of them has perished. NIV

Praise is the powerful tool that causes our faith to stay focused on what we know to be true and not on what is going on around us. This knowledge is what the Lord is referring to in the scriptures. "…and they will know the truth and the truth will set them free…" (Paraphrased) Real praise will put an atmosphere around you that will cause whatever is attacking you to back off.

R – IN PRAISE STANDS FOR **RELEASING GOD'S POWER…**

In Acts 16 Paul and Silas were beaten and thrown into the inner prison and told to be guarded by the chief jailer…

Now here's the power of God in the story… when they came to, Paul and Silas didn't complain or cry out in the confusion of why and how come! They raised their voices in praise and sang unto the Lord a new song… a song of praise… the whole jail was listening and so was God. Suddenly the Spirit of the Lord left heaven and entered the prison cell. Praise produced and released God's power!

A – IN PRAISE STANDS FOR **ACCESS TO THE PRESENCE OF GOD!**

Rom 5:1-6
1 Therefore, since we have been justified through faith, we have peace with God through our Lord Jesus Christ,
2 through whom we have gained access by faith into this grace in which we now stand. And we rejoice in the hope of the glory of God.

3 Not only so, but we also rejoice in our sufferings, because we know that suffering produces perseverance;
4 perseverance, character; and character, hope.
5 And hope does not disappoint us, because God has poured out his love into our hearts by the Holy Spirit, whom he has given us.
6 You see, at just the right time, when we were still power-less...NIV

Praise gives us access to His presence!

I – IN PRAISE STANDS FOR **INCREASES YOUR CAPACITY TO RECEIVE FROM GOD.**

Praise builds your faith! Learn to press in when you feel the anointing of God and shout out your praise. Don't let anyone stop you from praising God. Praise increases your capacity to receive... there were many people who would have never received from the Lord in the Gospel if they didn't cry their praises out loud to the Lord.

When Jesus noticed them... he didn't notice them because of what was troubling them. Jesus noticed them because their praise stood out in a crowd! Their shouts lasted longer than those around them and Jesus stopped to notice them because of their praises!

S – IN PRAISE STANDS FOR **SUSTAINING IN TOUGH TIMES!**

Praise will hold you up when everything else around you is failing you. You can find more strength in praise than in some-one trying to help you through your trial.

Praise brings out the joy of the Lord that's in you. The Word says that there is a greater source in you than what's in the world. God the Holy Spirit begins to break through the natural realm of understanding through the attitude of praise!

Praise will hold you long enough until your miracle can break through.

Ps 119:116
116 Sustain me according to your promise, and I will live; do not let my hopes be dashed. NIV

Ps 119:175
175 Let me live that I may praise you, and may your laws sustain me. NIV

Isa. 46:4
4 Even to your old age and gray hairs I am he, I am he who will sustain you. I have made you and I will carry you; I will sustain you and I will rescue you. NIV

E – IN PRAISE STANDS FOR ESTABLISHED AND ENCOURAGED

Praise will establish your identity in the Lord. When you are facing things that cause you to question who and what you're all about… praise will set your feet on the rock of revelation. You will begin to build your confidence. That confidence will not exist in what you can do but in what God can do. Praise will establish your faith and thus encourage you to hang on.

When David was in Ziglag he lost everything that was dear to him, his wives, his children, his livestock and all his materials.

The Word of the Lord tells us what David did to cope with his loss. He encouraged himself in the Lord!

David understood that if he didn't establish in himself that he is of God and that he belongs to God he would never get back what was stolen. Praise gives us the ability to see things in different scenery or setting. When we learn the art of real worship and praise we'll always see things through the eyes of faith and not fear, nor through the eyes of defeat and loss...

After David encouraged himself he sought the Lord in what to do. David wanted to know, should he pursue the enemy or not. If the instructions from the Lord were to pursue... David wanted to know what he could expect in his pursuit!

God told David to go and pursue the enemy and when he got there expect to get it all back. Praise will give us the assurance that, no matter what the enemy has stolen, when we move forward we will get back what the enemy has stolen. Here's the good news... not half or some... we will get it all back!

The right kind of praise will slap the devil in the face and cause you to survive whatever you're in and keep you lifted until God can work on your behalf to make the devil pay!

Conclusion

There was so much I could have written about on the faithfulness of God. This book is by no means an exhaustive list or study on the F.O.G. (faithfulness of God)

My intentions are to strike an interest in you on the nature and character of God so that you the reader will begin to develop a curiosity in pursuing The Lord Jesus Christ.

God is not a mean and awful God. He is not angry with us and doesn't desire to destroy us. The Word tells us that God is slow to anger and quick to forgive. God understands better than we do about the law of process. He himself took seven days to create what could have only taken Him a moment. God wanted to teach us the law of process.

Not everything in our lives has to be complete or perfect for it to be good. In the creation process of the world, God would look at what was done at the end of each day, and though it wasn't complete or perfect, he would say, "that is good." It's still good! It's good because it is in the process of what it's supposed to be.

God has been and always will be faithful to His words. Never allow anyone or anything to steer you from the fact that we serve an awesome and faithful God.

I hope and pray that this book was a blessing to you… it was an honor for me to write it and to share it with you.

If you ever need help in anyway and can't find anyone around who cares enough to take the time to help, look up to heaven! There is a faithful and merciful God who is eager to help and will!

In my third F.O.G. book Daddy God you can gain knowledge of what a wonderful daddy we have in heaven.

Stay close to the flame of His presence and remember no one is capable of satisfying you like the Holy Spirit can.

Walk in the F.O.G. (favor of God)
FOGMAN

Decision Page

*May I Invite You To Make Jesus
Christ The Lord Of Your Life?*

The Bible says, *"That if you will confess with your mouth the Lord Jesus, and will believe in your heart that God raised Him from the dead, you will be saved. For with the heart man believes unto righteousness; and with the mouth confession is made for salvation."* Romans 10:9,10

Pray this prayer with me today:
*"Dear Jesus, I believe that you died for me and rose again on the third day. I confess to you that I am a sinner. I need your love and forgiveness. Come into my life, forgive my sins and give me eternal life. I confess you now as my Lord. Thank you for my salvation! I walk in your peace and joy from this day forward. **Amen!"***

Signed _____

Date _____

[Return this Page today to an Usher or mail it in.]

Yes, BishopJerry! I made a decision to accept Christ as my personal Savior today. Please send me my free gift, to help me with my journey.

Name _____

Address _____

City _____ **State** _____ **Zip** _____

Phone _____ **Birth Date** _____

The Fog Zone Ministry
P.O. Box 3707, Hickory N.C. 28603
(828) 325- 4773   Fax:(828) 325-4877
www. Lwfword.com or email thefogzone@aol.com

We believe in the power of partnership. Everyone needs someone to partner with.

Your needs are important to us. Write us and we will put you in our F.O.G. Prayer Book. Let us hear from you when you have a spiritual need or are experiencing a conflict in your life.

Write to us and we will pray for your needs.

Bishop Jerry and Staff, please enter into the prayer of agreement with me for the following needs.

(Please Print)

_____

_____

_____

_____

_____

_____

_____

_____

SPECIAL THANKS

To my faithful and dedicated wife, Maryann, who puts up with all my craziness. Maryann, you are a source of blessing and inspiration. I couldn't have accomplished anything if I hadn't had you by my side. Thanks!

To my wonderful children, Jerry III and Jordan… daddy loves you greatly.

To my Dad and Mom, you have been wonderful parents and your legacy is great.

To Mike Murdock, for your inspiration and mentorship. Dr. Mike, you have been a spiritual father to me and I will never forget it. You have honored me! I will always be dedicated to supporting your visions and dreams.

To Living Word Family, Maryann and I are blessed and honored to be the senior pastors over this church. Thanks for all your patience in allowing me to grow at my own pace.

To Patricia and Leigh for proofreading all my mess and mistakes and for taking the time to help me write this book.

Thanks to Richard and Sharon Hart for believing in me and investing your special love and resources to make this project possible. I will always be grateful for your love and friendship. I know that God has put you into my life to be a Boaz. Thanks for listening to His voice.

Thanks to all the Pastors who let me come and preach on the

F.O.G.

Last, but not least... I saved the best for last.

TO MY WONDERFUL LORD... WHERE WOULD I BE
WITHOUT YOU? YOU HAVE BEEN THERE WHEN I
HAVE FALLEN... YOU HAVE BEEN THERE WHEN I
HAVE FAILED... YOU ARE TRUE TO YOUR WORD.

LORD, NO ONE COMPARES TO YOU. WHEN OTHERS
DIDN'T BELIEVE IN ME YOU DID!
WHEN OTHERS LEFT ME FOR DEAD, YOU RAISED
ME. WHEN HELL TRIED TO KILL ME, YOU STOOD
BETWEEN DEATH AND ME.

I AM SO BLESSED TO HAVE ACCEPTED YOU AS MY
LORD AND SAVIOR... MY COVENANT WITH YOU
STILL STANDS. TOGETHER WE WILL PULL PEOPLE
OUT OF HOLES.

THANKS LORD!